Illustrator:
Bruce Hedges

Editor:
Mary Kay Taggart

Editorial Project Manager:
Karen J. Goldfluss, M.S. Ed.

Editor in Chief:
Sharon Coan, M.S. Ed.

Creative Director:
Elayne Roberts

Art Coordination Assistant:
Cheri Macoubrie Wilson

Associate Designer:
Denise Bauer

Cover Artist:
Denise Bauer

Product Manager:
Phil Garcia

Imaging:
James Edward Grace

Publishers:
Rachelle Cracchiolo, M.S. Ed.
Mary Dupuy Smith, M.S. Ed.

Jumbo Book of Games

Over 250 games to energize the mind and body

Playground Games
quick and easy games
tag games
races and relays
ball games

Holiday Games
games for over a dozen holidays

Rainy-Day Games
sponge activities
just for fun games
curriculum–related games

International Games
more than 30 games from around the world

Authors:

Patti Sima, Fran Thompson, and Neal Jacob

With contributions by:

Cindy Postler, Donna Miriani, and Jeff Sima

Teacher Created Materials, Inc.
6421 Industry Way
Westminster, CA 92683
www.teachercreated.com

©*1999 Teacher Created Materials, Inc.*
Reprinted, 1999

Made in U.S.A.
ISBN-1-57690-099-1

Teacher Created Materials

The classroom teacher may reproduce copies of materials in this book for classroom use only. The reproduction of any part for an entire school or school system is strictly prohibited. No part of this publication may be transmitted, stored, or recorded in any form without written permission from the publisher.

Table of Contents

Table of Contents *(cont.)*

Table of Contents *(cont.)*

Table of Contents *(cont.)*

Introduction

The games children play offer an excellent opportunity for growth and learning. This book includes games for both indoor and outdoor enjoyment. You will find games in subject areas such as math, science, and language arts, as well as multicultural games to be enjoyed by all children. There is also an assortment of games for a variety of holidays throughout the year. The game pages can be easily photocopied onto thick paper or cardstock and laminated. These can then be stored in an open file box for easy access. Whenever you are in need of a game, you or your students can refer to the file for ideas. These game cards can be used year after year.

The following features of this book will aid in implementing the games:

- lists of required materials and equipment
- games for quiet times
- a multicultural focus
- games for many ages and skill levels
- a bibliography
- an index

This book is divided into four main sections:

Playground Games
Rainy-Day Games
Holiday Games
International Games

The games in this book combine mental and physical skills. Games may be used to teach good sportsmanship, fairness, taking turns, and a number of other personal and social values. As a leader of these games, you have the opportunity to provide guidance and supervision to see that all of the children are included and get the most out of their experiences.

You can help the children learn the following skills:

- the importance of cooperation
- to improve decision making skills in situations that require quick thinking
- to take turns and be patient
- to accept and follow rules
- to accept winning and losing gracefully
- to enjoy physical fitness

Introduction (cont.)

Tips for Leading Games

1. Use whatever materials are at hand (improvise).

2. Change or modify the rules to fit the situation.

3. Vary the activities.

4. Avoid situations where the children pick the teams.

5. Arrange the teams so that they are equal in skill level.

6. Instead of eliminating players from a game, give the opposing team a point.

7. Choose games that allow the children to be active most of the time.

8. Explain the rules of new outdoor games to the entire group in a confined area before going outside.

9. Have all of the equipment ready and the play area determined before beginning.

10. Do not tolerate teasing or unsportsmanlike behavior.

Playground Games

Spud

Equipment:
- playground ball

Where to Play:
outdoors

Number of Players:
six or more

Directions:

Assign each player a number. Do not duplicate the numbers, and number consecutively. Have the players form a circle. Choose one player to stand in the center, holding the ball. This player calls out a number and throws the ball into the air. The player whose number was called tries to catch the ball while the other players run away in any direction. When the player whose number was called has possession of the ball, he or she yells "Spud." When Spud is called, all of the players must stop running and freeze. The player with the ball may take three steps toward any player and attempt to hit that player by throwing the ball. If the player is hit below the waist, he or she gets a letter toward the spelling of "Spud." If the ball misses, the person who threw the ball gets the letter. The person who received a letter throws the ball during the next round. The first player to receive all four of the letters that spell Spud loses.

Skin the Snake

Equipment:
- none

Where to Play:

indoors or outdoors

Number of Players:

any large number, with six to eight players per team

Directions:

This can be done as a relay with the teams competing to finish first as a cooperative group activity. Each player passes his or her right hand back between his or her legs and using the left hand, grasps the right hand of the player in front. Without dropping hands, the last player of each team lies on the floor at full length. The rest of the players walk over the player on the floor, walking with one foot on each side of his or her body. When the first player to do this has gone back about as far as the last player's shoulder, he or she lies down so that the rest of the line can walk over both of them in the same fashion. Each player in turn lies on the floor, always keeping his or her hands clasped and feet close to the preceding player's body. As soon as every player is lying down, the last player to lie down rises and begins walking over the rest of the line, pulling the players to their feet.

Note: Do not do this activity if any of the participants are wearing skirts or dresses.

Midnight

Equipment:

• none

Where to Play:

an open area

Number of Players:

five or more

Directions:

Choose one player to be the fox. The fox stands at one end of the playing area in his or her "den." The rest of the players are chickens. They begin the game on the other end in the area known as the "chicken coop." To begin play, the chickens come out of their coop, walk up to the fox's den, and say "What time is it, Mr. (or Ms.) Fox?" The fox responds by saying any time, for example, 3:00. When the fox says, "Midnight," he or she runs out of the den and chases the chickens as they try to get back to their coop. Any chickens caught must go back to the fox's den and become foxes. Only Mr. (or Ms.) Fox will be allowed to say what time it is, but the new foxes may help chase the chickens. The last chicken left is the winner.

Steal the Bacon

Equipment:
- an object to represent the bacon

Where to Play:

in an open area, indoors or outdoors

Number of Players:

an even number of at least 10 players

Directions:

Form two lines about 15 feet (4.6 m) apart, facing each other. Number the lines, starting from the opposite ends. There should be an equal number of players on each side. If this is not possible, assign one player two numbers. Place the "bacon" in the center between the two lines. Call out a number, and those players whose number was called come out, try to take the bacon, and run back to their lines without being tagged. If a player makes it back to the line with the bacon without being tagged, that team is awarded two points. If the other team tags the person with the bacon before he or she reaches the line, that team is awarded one point. Play continues until one team reaches 10 points or for a predetermined amount of time.

	Formation	
10		1
9		2
8		3
7		4
6	bacon	5
5		6
4		7
3		8
2		9
1		10

12

© *Teacher Created Materials, Inc.*

Tunnel Race

Equipment:
- none

Where to Play:

a large area

Number of Players:

an odd number of 11 or more players

Directions:

Select one player to be "it." Divide the remaining players into two circles. Direct one circle to stand around the other. The people in the inside circle should face the people in the outside circle. The people in each circle should then take the hands of the people they are facing so that the entire circle forms a tunnel of pairs. The player who was chosen as "it" walks through the tunnel, tags any pair, and then steps into one of their spaces. Then, the two tagged players each run in opposite directions until they return to their original spots. The first person to return will be able to slip into the remaining space. The last person to get there will be "it" for the next round.

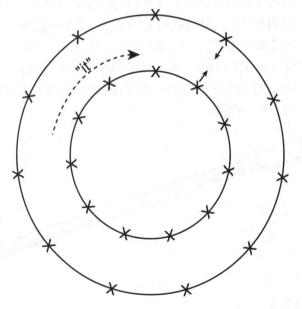

Dogcatcher

Equipment:
- none

Where to Play:

a large, open area

Number of Players:

six or more

Directions:

Select one person to be the dogcatcher. Choose three types of dogs to be the teams, for example, German shepherds, poodles, and Dalmatians. Assign each player to a dog team. Line up the dogs on one end of the playing area, and designate a line on the opposite end of the area. Play begins when the dogcatcher calls out the name of one type of dog. The goal of the players who have been assigned to that dog team is to run across the playing area and to cross the line at the other end without being tagged. If a dog is tagged, he or she becomes a dogcatcher and must help to catch the other dogs.

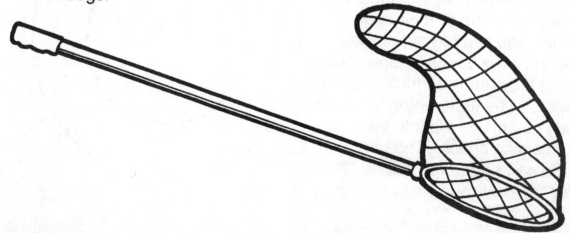

Octopus

Equipment:
- a soft, spongy ball

Where to Play:

a large, open, grassy area

Number of Players:

at least six

Directions:

Select one player to be the octopus. The rest of the players will be fish. Designate a goal at each end of the playing area. Give the octopus a ball to tag or hit the fish with. When the octopus calls out "Fish, fish, swim in my ocean," the fish must attempt to "swim" across the "ocean" to the opposite goal. If a fish gets tagged or hit by the ball, he or she freezes, facing in the direction he or she was running. All of the players who have been tagged become tentacles in the remaining rounds. The tentacles may not move from their spots, but they may wave their arms around to try to tag the fish. The last fish in the game is the winner.

Rock, Paper, Scissors Tag

Equipment:
 • none

Where to Play:
a large, open area

Number of Players:
four or more

Directions:

This game is a variation of the classic Rock, Paper, Scissors. In the original version, a closed fist represents a rock, a hand held flat is paper, and two extended fingers represent scissors. The players face each other, and each person hits his or her open palm with the other fist while chanting "Rock, paper, scissors." On the next beat each player forms one of the three symbols. Paper beats a rock, a rock breaks (beats) scissors, and scissors cut (beats) paper.

To play the tag version of this game, divide the players into two teams. Designate a safety zone for each team and a line in the center at which the teams can meet.

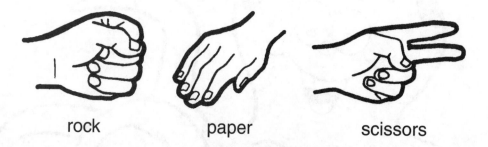

rock   paper   scissors

Rock, Paper, Scissors Tag *(cont.)*

Before each round, the teams need to meet individually to each choose one of the three symbols. Then the teams face each other in two lines, and together say "rock, paper, scissors," and display their symbols. The team that displays the winning symbol chases the other team, trying to tag their players before they reach their safety zone. Any tagged players will then join the opposing team. Play until one of the teams has been eliminated or until a designated time period is over. The team with the most people wins.

Paper beats rock.

Scissors beats paper.

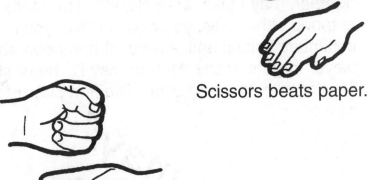

Rock beats scissors

Mother, May I?

Equipment:
- none

Where to Play:

any open area

Number of Players:

four or more

Directions:

Choose a player to be Mother and designate the starting and finishing lines for the players. The players line up at the starting line, facing Mother who is at the finishing line. Players take turns asking Mother if they may move forward in any way they choose. For example, a player may ask "Mother, may I take three baby steps?" or "Mother, may I take three skips?" The Mother has the option to respond either "Yes, you may," or "No, you may not." The player continues asking until a request has been answered with a yes. If a player forgets to say "Mother may I?" he or she must go back to the starting line and start over. The first player to reach Mother is the winner.

"Yes, you may."

"No, you may not."

Red Light, Green Light

Equipment:
- none

Where to Play:

a large, open area

Number of Players:

four or more

Directions:

Choose a player to be the traffic signal. Designate a start line and a finish line. The players line up at the start line, facing the traffic signal who is standing at the finish line. The traffic signal turns his or her back to the players and says "Green light." At this time the players run forward toward the traffic signal. After the traffic signal says "Red light," the players must freeze, and the traffic signal quickly turns around to face the players. If he or she sees any of the players still moving, they must go back to the start line. The first player to make it to the finish line and tag the traffic signal becomes the new traffic signal.

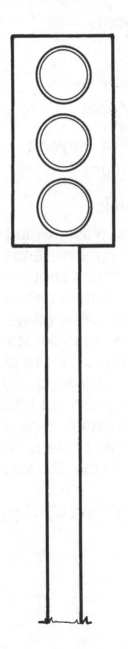

Red Rover

Equipment:
- none

Where to Play:

a grassy area

Number of Players:

eight or more

Directions:

Divide the players into two teams of equal size. Have the teams line up at the opposite ends of the playing field. Choose a team to go first. The team should choose one player from the opposing team that they want to call over. Then they join hands and call "Red Rover, Red Rover, send (player's name) right over!" The player who is called then runs across the field and tries to break through the clasped hands of two players. If he or she breaks through, a player from the team which is holding hands must go to the other team. If the player does not break through, he or she must join the team that is holding hands. The teams take turns at this process until one team has all of the players. If you are playing for a designated amount of time, the team with the most players wins.

"Red Rover, Red Rover, send Cindy right over!"

Head and Shoulders, Knees and Toes

Equipment:
- none

Where to Play:

anywhere

Number of Players:

two or more

Directions:

This is a good warm-up activity. Lead everyone in singing the following song:

"Head and shoulders, knees and toes, knees and toes. Head and shoulders, knees and toes, oh-oh-oh-oh-oh. Eyes and ears and nose and mouth . . . head and shoulders, knees and toes, knees and toes!"

As the players sing along, they use their hands to touch the body parts that they are naming. Increase the speed of the song and movements to make it more exciting.

Elbow to Elbow

Equipment:
- none

Where to Play:

an open area

Number of Players:

four or more

Directions:

Have the players pair off. Those without a partner may report to you so that you can then find them a partner or create a trio. Chant "Elbow to elbow." As you do, have the pairs touch their elbows to each other. Then try other combinations such as "Knees to knees," "Ear to shoulder," "Hand to toes," and so on. With every combination that you call, the players should attempt to match the body parts. This is a good lead-in activity for other games that require partners.

Calling All Cars

Equipment:
- none

Where to Play:

a large, open area

Number of Players:

four or more

Directions:

This game is better suited for younger children. Count off the children by fours: 1, 2, 3, 4; 1, 2, 3, 4; etc. Place all of the ones in one corner, all of the twos in another corner, and so on. Describe the need for a police officer's help, and say "Calling police, calling police . . . car number _____, car number_____." Insert one, two, three, or four as the car number. The children who are in that number group will then leave their corner and run around the room once or twice (or as many times as you decide) and then return to their corner. Repeat the sequence. Try calling two police car numbers at one time, or shout "Calling all cars, calling all cars!" Continue until the children's interest begins to drift.

Ghosts in the Graveyard

Equipment:
- none

Where to Play:

a large, open area

Number of Players:

at least four

Directions:

This is a good cool-down activity. Choose one person to be the leader. The leader says "Ghosts in the graveyard . . . 5-4-3-2-1-freeze!" At this point the players need to lie still. (The leader stands throughout the game.) If the leader sees a person move, he or she says "Got you, (player's name)." The player who moved then has to help the leader find other moving players in the remaining rounds. The last player left is the winner. This is usually an elimination game, but you may prefer to allow the children who get caught moving to join the game again after one or two rounds.

24

© *Teacher Created Materials, Inc.*

Birds in a Nest

Equipment:
- none

Where to Play:

a large, open area

Number of Players:

at least 14

Directions:

Choose one player to be a cat and another to be a bird who does not have a nest. Divide the remaining players into groups of three. Have two of the members of each group join hands to make a tree. The third person in each group is the bird who stands under the limbs of the tree (the arms of the partners). The one player who is the bird without a nest runs from the cat to a tree. The bird who is in that tree has to vacate it and become the bird without a nest. He or she must run from the cat to another tree. If the cat catches a bird, the roles are reversed—the cat becomes a bird, and the bird becomes a cat.

Lion, May We Cross Your River?

Equipment:
- none

Where to Play:

a large, open area, indoors or outdoors

Number of Players:

four or more

Directions:

Choose one player to be the lion. The other players line up on the opposite side of the playing area from the lion and say "Lion, may we cross your river?" The lion responds "Yes, if you are wearing . . .," and he or she says a color. The players wearing that color may run to the opposite line safely. However, the players who are not wearing the color may be tagged by the lion while trying to cross the line. Players who are tagged are out. Play continues until there is only one player left.

Monkey in the Middle

Equipment:
- none

Where to Play:

an open area

Number of Players:

three

Directions:

One player is chosen to be the monkey. He or she stands in the middle of two players who are standing approximately 10 feet (3 m) apart, facing each other. The two players throw the ball to each other while the monkey tries to intercept it. If the monkey gets the ball, the last person to have touched the ball becomes the new monkey.

Army, Navy

Equipment:
• none

Where to Play:
a large playing field

Number of Players:
nine or more

Directions:
Choose one person to be the caller. Divide the rest of the players into two teams, Army and Navy. Have the teams line up at the opposite ends of the field. The caller can call out any of the following: "Army, hit the deck," "Navy, hit the deck," "Army, take off," or "Navy, take off." If "hit the deck" is called, players on that team should drop to the ground on their stomachs. The last person to drop is eliminated. If "take off" is called, players on that team should run to the opposite end of the field. The last person to reach the end of the field is out. Play continues until only one person on each team is remaining.

"Navy, hit the deck."

"Army, take off."

Contrary Children

Equipment:
- none

Where to Play:

an open area

Number of Players:

five or more

Directions:

This game is the opposite of Simon Says. Players are to do the opposite of what they are told. For example, if the caller says "Wave your left hand," players should wave their right hands, or when told "Take two steps away from me," the players should take two steps toward the caller. Players are eliminated when they are caught doing what they are told to do instead of the opposite. The last player remaining is the winner.

"Wave your left hand"

Hide and Seek

Equipment:
- none

Where to Play:

any large area with a lot of places to hide

Number of Players:

three or more

Directions:

Select one player to be "it." Determine what the boundaries will be, and choose a place to be home base. "It" stands at home base with eyes covered and counts to 100. While he or she is counting, the other players scatter to their hiding places. "It" then announces "Ready or not, here I come," and leaves home base in search of the other players. While he or she is looking for the hidden players, they may make a run for home base. If they reach home base without being tagged by "it," they are safe. The first player to be tagged is "it" in the next round.

"Ready or not, here I come."

Kitty Wants a Corner

Equipment:
- none

Where to Play:

an area that you can mark off with four corners

Number of Players:

five or more

Directions:

The player chosen to be the kitty stands in the center while the other players stand in the corners. The kitty says "Kitty wants a corner," and all of the players, including the kitty, must run to new corners. The last player to get to a corner becomes the new kitty.

Guard the Pin

Equipment:

- a rubber ball

- a bowling pin (or similar object)

Where to Play:

indoors or outdoors

Number of Players:

10 to 15 per circle

Directions:

Place the pin in the middle of the circle. Choose one player to be in the center of each circle. The person in the center tries to guard the pin while the rest of the players in the circle try to knock it down with the ball. The player who knocks down the pin will be in the center for the next game.

Statues

Equipment:
- none

Where to Play:

outdoors, on a grassy area

Number of Players:

more than four

Directions:

The player designated as the twirler takes one player at a time by the hand, twirls him or her around twice, and then lets go. The person swung around freezes in a pose until the other players have all been swung into statue poses. The twirler selects one statue at a time to come to life and then the twirler chooses a favorite to become the twirler for the next round.

Variation: The twirler can set up a category for the poses ahead of time, such as animals or occupations.

Capture the Flag

Equipment:
- a scarf or bandanna for each team

Where to Play:

an outdoor area

Number of Players:

at least eight

Directions:

Divide the playing area into two equal sides. Designate a prison area on each side. Hang one flag (a scarf or bandanna) on each side. The flag must be visible from 50 feet (15.24 m) away, and no defenders may hide within 20 feet (6.09 m) of it. Some players will defend their flag while others will go into enemy territory and try to capture the opponent's flag and safely bring it to the other side. If a player is tagged in enemy territory, he or she is taken to the prison. The prisoner can be rescued when a team member breaks through and tags him or her. Both get to return safely to their side. The game ends when the enemy's flag is captured or all of one side has been taken prisoner.

The States Game

Equipment:
- a newspaper

Where to Play:

any area large enough for students to form a circle

Number of Players:

any number, but a large group is better

Directions:

Arrange the players in a circle, and have each one choose the name of a state and tell it to the other players. Select one player to be "it." "It" takes a rolled-up newspaper, stands in the middle of the circle, and calls out the name of a state. The person with the name of that state calls out another person's state, who then calls another state, and so on. The "it" player tries to tap another player on the shoulder with the newspaper when the player's state has been called but before he or she has had a chance to think of another player's state. If a player fails to name a state or names a state that isn't being used and gets tapped with the newspaper, that player becomes "it," and the former "it" takes a place in the circle.

Four-Person Circle Chase

Equipment:
* none

Where to Play:
any area large enough to form a circle

Number of Players:
12 to 16

Directions:
Arrange the players in a circle, and count them off in fours: 1, 2, 3, 4; 1, 2, 3, 4; etc. Choose a leader to call out a number from one to four. Each player whose number is called (there will be several) runs around the circle in the same direction and tries to tag the player in front of him or her. The tagged players are out, and the remaining runners try to tag the next runners in front of them until they reach their original positions in the circle. The leader then calls another number, and the procedure is repeated. When all of the numbers have been called, the remaining players start over with new numbers. This continues until only four players remain and are named the winners.

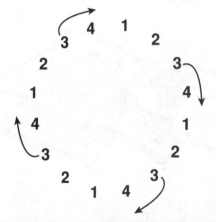

Leapfrog

Equipment:
- none

Where to Play:

outdoors

Number of Players:

six or more

Directions:

Designate a start and a finish line. Divide the players into two teams. One player from each team should squat down at the start line while the rest of the players line up, single file, approximately six feet (1.82 m) behind him or her. The first player in line for each team runs up to the player squatted down and vaults over him or her. The next player in line vaults over both players, one at a time. This continues until all of the players have leapfrogged over the others; then, the first player to have been jumped over gets up and jumps over the rest. The team that reaches the finish line first wins.

Sardines

Equipment:

- none

Where to Play:

a large, open area

Number of Players:

five or more

Directions:

This game is the opposite of Hide-and-Seek. The players all stand with their backs to the playing area. Choose one player to go first to find a hiding place that is large enough to fit all of the other players. Once the chosen player is hidden, the rest of the players search for him or her. When they find the hidden player, they join him or her in the hiding spot. Soon there are several players packed into the hiding spot like sardines. The game ends when the last player discovers the hiding spot.

Simon Says

Equipment:
- none

Where to Play:

indoors or outdoors

Number of Players:

four or more

Directions:

Choose one player to be Simon. Simon faces the rest of the players and gives an instruction while demonstrating it. If the instruction begins with the words "Simon says . . . ," then the players must follow the command. If Simon issues a command without the words "Simon says . . . ," then the players who follow the command are out. For example, the leader says, "Simon says, 'Pat your head.' " The players should pat their heads. However, if the leader just says "Pat your head," without the command "Simon says . . . ," any player who pats his or her head is eliminated. The winner is the last player who follows instructions without getting eliminated.

Barnyard Peanut Hunt

Equipment:
- 1 or 2 pounds (.45 or .91 kg) of unshelled peanuts
- a small bag for each team

Where to Play:
a large room, suitable for hiding peanuts

Number of Players:
a minimum of 12

Directions:
Before starting the game, hide the peanuts around the room. Divide the teams into groups of at least three. Ask the groups to each select a captain and a type of animal. At the sound of the start signal, the teams begin searching for the peanuts. The captains are the only ones allowed to hold the bags and pick up the peanuts. When a non-captain player finds a peanut, he or she imitates the sound of the team's animal to get the captain to come over and pick up the peanut. At the end of a predetermined search period, the team with the most peanuts is the winner.

Circle Golf

Equipment:
- a golf ball

- a small golf club, a croquet mallet, or a stiff yardstick

- a plastic cup or jar

- string

Where to Play:

outside

Number of Players:

two or more

Directions:

Using string, mark off a circle about 6 feet (1.82 meters) in diameter in the grass. Choose one spot as 12 o'clock and place the cup there (either dig a small hole for it or lay it on its side). One at a time, the players will putt from the 1 o'clock position to the 12 o'clock position. Have each player keep track of the number of strokes it takes to complete the circle and get his or her ball in the cup. The player who completes the circle in the fewest number of strokes is the winner.

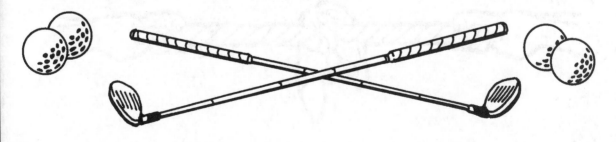

Tug of War

Equipment:
- a long, smooth, sturdy rope

- a bandanna or rag

Where to Play:
outside, on grass

Number of Players:
a minimum of six

Directions:

Divide the players into two teams of approximately equal size and strength. Establish a center line in the pulling area. Have the teams line up, single file, on either side of the rope, and then tie the bandanna around the exact middle point of the rope. Have the players position themselves a few feet apart, and place the bigger or stronger team members at the ends to serve as anchors. At the signal "Go!" both teams attempt to pull the first member of the other team across the center line. The team that succeeds in doing this is the winner.

Push of War

Equipment:
- a large medicine ball

Where to Play:

a gymnasium or grassy field

Number of Players:

four or more

Directions:

Divide the players into two equal teams and have them stand at the opposite ends of the playing area. Place the ball in the center. At the sound of the starting signal, the teams rush toward the ball and try to advance it by pushing or punching it with their hands. Kicking and carrying the ball are not allowed. A team scores a point when they push the ball past their opponent's goal line. The winner is the team who is ahead at the end of a predetermined amount of time.

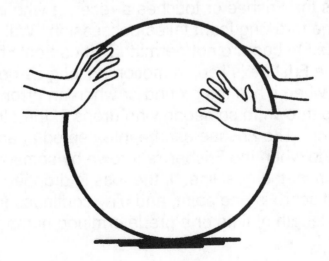

Ultimate Frisbee

Equipment:
- one Frisbee

Where to Play:

a large, grassy field

Number of Players:

a minimum of six

Directions:

The playing area should be around 180 feet long and 90 feet wide (54.8 x 27.4 meters), but it can be shortened, depending on how many people are playing. Form two equal teams and have them each line up behind their own goal lines. The game begins when the throwing team tosses the Frisbee to the receiving team. The receivers can catch it and begin moving it down the field or let it land untouched and then begin to move it. If a member of the throwing team intercepts the Frisbee or touches a receiver who is about to catch it, then the throwing team takes possession. Walking and running with the Frisbee are not permitted. It can only be advanced by passing. The Frisbee is kept in motion as long as possible, only coming to rest when it hits the ground or when an error is committed. If the Frisbee is thrown to someone who drops it, the other team gains possession. The Frisbee can be intercepted at any time. Scores are made when the Frisbee is thrown by someone in the field to a teammate past the goal line. If the toss is dropped, possession changes. Each score is one point, and play continues for a predetermined length of time or a predetermined number of points.

Obstacle Course

Equipment:
- varies according to the objects available and the location of the course (suggestions: natural obstacles, tires, jump ropes, boxes, etc.)

Where to Play:
a large, open area

Number of Players:
three or more

Directions:
The obstacles can be as easy or as complicated as you wish to make them. If you are using a playground, utilize the equipment already available, such as the swings and monkey bars. Obstacles can also be created. For example, a jump rope can be tied between two trees as a hurdle or used for jumping a certain number of times. Use your imagination and creativity when setting up the course. Before beginning, demonstrate the course by walking through it for the players so that they know what is expected at each station. Players should be timed, and the player with the fastest time is the winner.

Egg Toss

Equipment:
- one hard-boiled egg for every two players

Where to Play:

outside

Number of Players:

four or more

Directions:

Divide the players into groups of two. Have partners line up facing each other, approximately 4 feet (1.2 m) apart. All of the eggs should be held by players on the same side. At the signal, the players holding the eggs gently throw the eggs to their partners. The players who have caught the eggs take a step back and at the next signal throw the eggs to their partners. When an egg falls and breaks, the pair is out. The last team left with an egg is the winner.

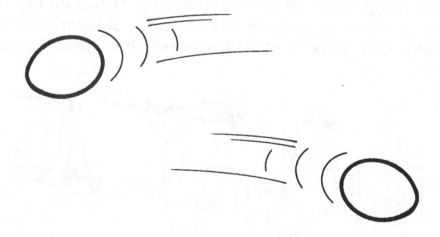

46

© Teacher Created Materials, Inc.

Ice Cubes

Equipment:
- one ice cube for each team

Where to Play:

anywhere, but ideally outside during warm weather

Number of Players:

six or more

Directions:

Divide the players into equal groups of two or three. The object of this game is to be the first team to melt the ice cube. At the starting signal, each team begins to attempt to melt its ice cube by rubbing it with their hands, passing it from player to player, etc. The only restrictions are that the ice cube cannot be put inside a player's mouth and cannot touch the ground. Also, it must be passed around. No player may keep it for more than five seconds before passing it on. The first team to melt its ice cube wins.

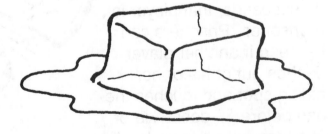

Kick the Can

Equipment:
- one aluminum can

Where to Play:

outside

Number of Players:

a minimum of five

Directions:

One player is designated "it" and begins the game by kicking the can as far as possible. As the can is rolling, the others run and hide. "It" then puts the can back in its original spot and counts to 50 to allow for more hiding time. "It" then yells out "Ready or not, here I come!" and goes looking for the others. When "it" sees someone, he or she calls out the player's name and runs back to touch the can before the newly discovered player does. If "it" succeeds, that player is a prisoner. Prisoners can be freed if another player dashes out of his or her hiding spot and touches the can before "it" does. He or she then yells "Home free!" and the captured players are free to hide again.

48

© *Teacher Created Materials, Inc.*

Beanbag Toss

Equipment:
- a beanbag
- paper
- pen
- tape or chalk

Where to Play:
indoors or outdoors

Number of Players:
a minimum of two

Directions:
Use chalk or tape to create a circular target on the ground. Assign point values to the parts of the target. Be creative in making the different patterns and point values. Have the players stand behind a tossing line and face the target. (When determining the line, take into account the players' ages and abilities.) The players take turns tossing the beanbag and accruing points. Keep track of the points with a pen and paper. Play for a specific number of rounds or up to a predetermined point total.

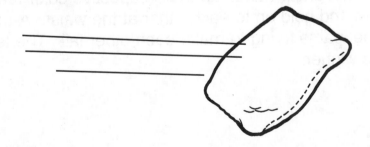

London Bridge

Equipment:
- none

Where to Play:

outdoors on a grassy area

Number of Players:

a minimum of eight

Directions:

Select two players to form the bridge, and ask them to secretly decide who will be gold and who will be silver. Have them face each other and join their hands up high to form a bridge. The rest of the players form a single line on one side of the bridge and sing:

London Bridge is falling down, falling down, falling down.

London Bridge is falling down, my fair lady.

At the words "my fair lady," the bridge people lower their arms and take prisoner the player in between them. The bridge people ask the prisoner to choose silver or gold. The prisoner then replaces the bridge person who has that color. Play continues until the last prisoner has been captured and chosen a color. The two original bridge people then grasp hands as their respective color teams line up behind them and hold on to each other at the waist. A tug of war ensues with the teams trying to make each other fall. The team left standing is the winner.

50

© Teacher Created Materials, Inc.

Potsie

Equipment:
- a bouncy ball
- chalk

Where to Play:

outdoors on a paved area

Number of Players:

two or more

Directions:

Using the chalk, draw a large rectangle on the pavement. The rectangle should be divided into six or eight boxes, each about one by two feet (30 by 60 cm). In each of the boxes, write the name of a category that is familiar to everyone. Number the boxes 1–6 or 1–8, depending on how many squares there are. The first player stands outside of the box and rolls the ball into the first square. He or she may use hands or feet to stop the ball before it rolls out of the box. If it rolls out, the player loses a turn. Before moving on to the next box, the player must name something from the box's category. For example, if the box is labeled "boys' names," the player may say, "Jeff." If a correct answer is given, the player moves to the next box. From the second box on, when entering a new box the player must bounce and catch the ball while giving a correct answer. If the player loses control of the ball or gives an incorrect answer, he or she loses a turn and passes play to the next player. Players may decide whether or not an incorrect answer will result in returning to the first square on the next turn or if the player may continue where he or she left off. The first player to make it through all of the boxes is the winner.

Balloon Bounce

Equipment:
- a balloon

- a paper cup of water for each player

- 20 toothpicks

- a large coat

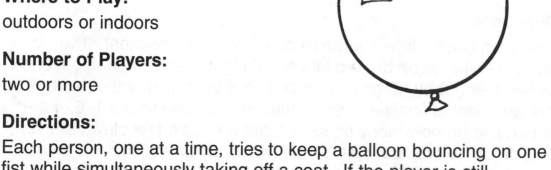

Where to Play:

outdoors or indoors

Number of Players:

two or more

Directions:

Each person, one at a time, tries to keep a balloon bouncing on one fist while simultaneously taking off a coat. If the player is still bouncing the balloon after taking the coat off, he or she must then pick up 20 toothpicks, one at a time. If the player is still bouncing the balloon, he or she must complete the last stunt, drinking a glass of water. As a tiebreaker, if more than one player accomplishes all of these stunts, the group can think up harder things to do while bouncing the balloon.

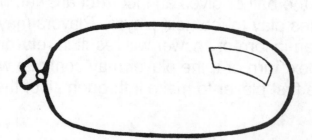

Mixed-Up Ball

Equipment:
- a kickball

Where to Play:

a large, open field

Number of Players:

eight or more

Directions:

This game is played like traditional kickball, except that the kicker and the runners must run in the direction in which the ball is kicked. For example, if the ball is kicked to the left side of the playing field, the kicker runs to what is traditionally third base, and any players on the bases also run in the direction opposite from what they are used to. Allow each player on a team to kick once and then switch sides. You may want to play for a predetermined amount of time or a certain number of innings.

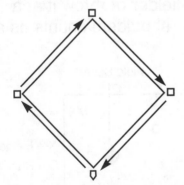

If the ball is kicked to the left of second base, the players run clockwise.

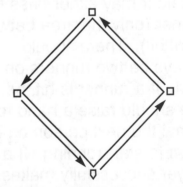

If the ball is kicked to the right of second base, the players run counterclockwise.

Field Dodge Ball

Equipment:
- a rubber ball

Where to Play:
baseball diamond/field

Number of Players:
eight or more

Directions:

Divide the players into two teams. One team will start as the runners while the other team fields. Teams switch positions after each player on the running team has run twice. Before beginning, have the fielding team spread out over the playing area while the running team lines up behind the home base line. The game starts when the leader rolls the ball onto the playing field. Two runners try to circle the field bases and return home without getting hit by the ball. The fielders may run to get the ball but must not move once they have it. A fielder may either pass the ball to another fielder or throw it at a runner (only the area between the knees and shoulders counts as a legal hit). There should always be two runners on the field. If a runner is hit, he or she should raise a hand to signal the next person on the team to start running. If a player successfully makes it to the home base line without being hit, the team scores one point.

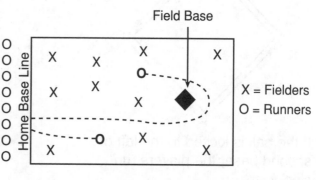

Three-Zone Football

Equipment:
- a football

Where to Play:
an open field

Number of Players:
eight or more

Directions:
Divide the playing area into three zones and an area for the quarterback. Award each zone a different point value. Zone one is worth one point, zone two is worth three points, and zone three is worth five points. Assign two offensive players and two defensive players to each zone. Allow the quarterback 10 seconds to throw the ball to a receiver in any of the zones. The defensive team tries to prevent the offensive players from catching the ball. Each team has four chances, or downs, to score as many points as possible, and then the teams change positions. If the defensive team intercepts the ball, the teams trade positions.

Quarterback

Zone 3	Zone 2	Zone 1		
x o	x o	x o	↓	
			o x	o = Offensive x = Defensive
x o	x o	x o		

California Kickball

Equipment:

- a kickball

- bases

Where to Play:

a kickball field

Number of Players:

10 or more

Directions:

Divide the group into two teams. Set up the bases as shown. This game is similar to regular kickball. There are two ways to make outs—by tagging a player or group of players or by catching the ball in the air. Unlike regular kickball, the players do not have to run when the ball is kicked. There is no limit to the number of players on any base. Any time the ball is kicked, one, some, or all of the players on a base may run to the next base, but if more than one player is running they must join hands. If the runners break apart, they must sit out, which counts as one out. If any member of the group is tagged, all of the members must sit out, but this only counts as one out. Each player to cross home base counts as one run. For example, a group of three counts as three points. Teams change sides after three outs. Play for a predetermined length of time or a certain number of innings.

☐ 3rd	☐ 2nd
☐ 4th	☐ 1st

Home

Throw, Kick, Run

Equipment:
- a football
- bases
- three cones

Where to Play:
an open area

Number of Players:
eight or more

Directions:
Divide the players into two teams. During his or her turn, each player on the offensive team either kicks or throws a football and runs back and forth between both bases as many times as possible. Meanwhile, the defensive team retrieves the ball and knocks down the three cones in order. The offensive player scores one point for each trip made between the bases during this time. The teams switch sides after every player has had a turn.

Cone 2 △ 　　　　　□
　　　　　　　　Base 2

　　　　　　　　　　　　　　　△ Cone 1

Cone 3 △

　　　　　　　　□
　　　　　　Base 1

Drop and Kick

Equipment:
- a kickball

Where to Play:
a large, open area

Number of Players:
eight or more

Directions:
Divide the players into two teams. A player on the offensive team drops the ball and kicks it. Then he or she attempts to run across the marker line and return to the home line without being hit by the ball. The fielders try to catch the ball and use it to hit the kicker while he or she is in the danger zone. If the kicker is hit while in the danger zone, it is considered an out. The teams change sides after every player has had a turn to kick. Two points are earned for every player who crosses the home line without being hit. One point is scored by the defensive team for catching a fly ball.

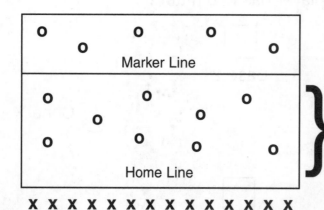

o = Fielder
x = Kicker

Freezer-Defroster Tag

Equipment:
  • none

Where to Play:
outside

Number of Players:
five or more

Directions:
In this version of tag, a player who is tagged by "it" must bend over and freeze in a position simulating a croquet hoop. The frozen player is not allowed to "defrost" until another player crawls through his or her hoop. The frozen player may then return to the game.

TV Tag

Equipment:
- none

Where to Play:

outside

Number of Players:

five or more

Directions:

There are two ways to play this game. One way is that a player must say the name of a television show when approached by "it." If he or she cannot think of one or says one that has already been said, then "it" can tag the player. This can be made more difficult by adding stipulations, such as it has to be a current show or a cartoon.

In the other way to play TV tag, "it" asks a player a question about television, such as "Who is the star of . . . ?" or "What channel is . . . on?" If the player can answer the question correctly, then he or she is saved. If the question is answered incorrectly, "it" can try to tag the player. When a player is tagged, he or she then becomes "it."

Bronco Tag

Equipment:
- none

Where to Play:
a large, open area

Number of Players:
10 or more

Directions:
Divide the players into groups of three or four. Select one player to be "it." Ask the groups to line up to form broncos. The first person in each group line will represent the head. The rest of the players will represent the body and will hold onto each other at the waist (forming a chain). The broncos begin running while "it" attempts to join onto the end of one of the broncos. If "it" succeeds in joining a bronco, then the head of that bronco becomes "it," and the next player in line becomes the new head.

Pompom Pull Away

Equipment:
- none

Where to Play:
outside

Number of Players:
six or more

Directions:

Choose one person to be "it." Divide the remaining players into two groups. Have the groups form two lines facing each other approximately 25 feet (7.6 m) apart. "It" stands in the middle of the playing area and calls "Pompom pull away, run away, catch away!" Meanwhile, the rest of the players try to run across the playing area without being tagged by "it." If a player is tagged, he or she must join "it" in the center. The last player to remain untagged wins.

Elbow Tag

Equipment:
   • none

Where to Play:
any large, open area

Number of Players:
seven or more

Directions:
Choose one player to be "it" and another to be a runner. The rest of the players pair up and link elbows with their partners. While they have their inside elbows linked, they should keep their outside elbows bent and their hands at their waists. The person who is "it" tries to tag the runner. The runner can avoid being tagged by linking an elbow with the free elbow of any player on the playing field. When a pair is joined by a runner, the partner whose elbow is free becomes the new runner and must run from "it" or join elbows with another pair. If a player is tagged by "it," the roles are reversed. You can experiment with this game by having the pairs arranged in a circle or placed randomly on the field. Partners can either face in the same direction or in opposite directions. Another variation is to have "it" be allowed to join a pair and release another player to be "it."

Everybody's It

Equipment:
   • none

Where to Play:
a large, open area

Number of Players:
three or more

Directions:

Everybody's It: This is a very quick tag game. There are only two rules . . . everybody is it, and a player who is tagged must freeze. The final player to remain unfrozen is the winner.

Option: Choose a player to be "it." The first time a player is tagged by "it," he or she must keep one hand on the place that was tagged. The next time, he or she must put the free hand on the place that was tagged the second time. After three tags the player must freeze. The last player to be frozen is "it" in the next round.

Rattlesnake Tag

Equipment:
• none

Where to Play:
a large, open area

Number of Players:
10 to 30

Directions:

Designate a 10 feet by 10 feet (3 m by 3 m) area to represent the snake's home. Choose one child to be the snake. The snake leaves its home and attempts to tag the children. When a player is tagged, he or she becomes part of the snake, and they must join hands and try to catch the other players. Any further tagged players must also join the snake by holding hands. The snake gradually grows in length by tagging people, using only the free hands of the players on its ends.

If the snake breaks apart (the players lose their grips on each other), the free player(s) then chase the snake back to its home where it is safe. However, before the snake reaches its home, the free player(s) may tag individual members of the snake, thereby freeing them. As soon as the snake reaches the safety of its home, the remaining members reassemble and start out again to tag the others. Play continues until there is only one player left who has not been caught.

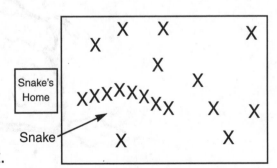

Blob

Equipment:
- none

Where to Play:
a large, open area

Number of Players:
six or more

Directions:
Set boundaries determined by the size of the group. Choose one player to be the Blob. When the Blob tags someone, that person joins hands with the Blob. Only the free hands on either side of the Blob may tag other players. Once the Blob has four or more members, it may split into groups of two or more and continue to tag players. The different Blobs may work together to chase and tag the remaining players. The winner is the last player who has not been tagged by a Blob. This person is the Blob for the next round.

Snow White and the Seven Dwarfs

Equipment:
• none

Where to Play:
a large, grassy area

Number of Players:
at least nine

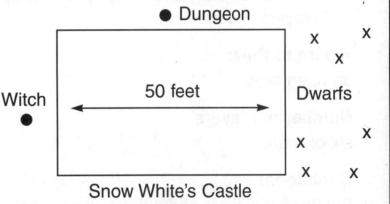

● Dungeon

Witch

50 feet

Dwarfs

Snow White's Castle

Directions:

Divide the players into seven groups. Give each group the name of one of the dwarfs (Grumpy, Bashful, Happy, Sneezy, Sleepy, Dopey, or Doc). Mark off a playing field approximately 50 feet (15.24 m) in length. Select one player to be Snow White and place him or her on the sideline in the castle. Choose another player to be the witch and place him or her at one end of the field. Place the dwarf teams at the opposite end of the field. The witch calls out the name of one of the dwarfs, and all of the members of that group run to the end of the playing field and back. The witch moves into the field and tries to tag the dwarfs as they run. Any players tagged by the witch are placed in the dungeon opposite Snow White's castle. Snow White may free the prisoners by crossing the playing space and tagging those in the dungeon. However, if the witch catches Snow White, the game is over and the witch wins. If, after 10 minutes of play, Snow White has not been caught and has kept the dungeon free of prisoners, Snow White and the dwarfs win.

Posture Tag

Equipment:
- two rectangular, loosely filled beanbags to mold to the top of the players' heads

Where to Play:

an open area

Number of Players:

six or more

Directions:

Scatter the players about the playing area. Ask for two players to volunteer, one to be "it" and the other to be chased. Each of the two players places a beanbag on top of his or her head. "It" starts to chase the other player. The players are not allowed to use their hands to keep the beanbags in place while running. The player being chased becomes "safe" by using his or her hands to place the beanbag on another player's head. That player may assist in the process. If the beanbag is successfully placed on another player's head, then "it" chases that person. Whenever "it" tags the other player, that player becomes "it" and chases the one who tagged him or her. If the beanbag falls off the head of the player being chased, that player automatically becomes "it" and the roles are reversed. If the beanbag falls off the head of "it," that player picks it up and continues as "it."

Chimp Race

Equipment:
 • none

Where to Play:
outdoors

Number of Players:
four or more

Directions:
Chose one player to be the starter and have him or her stand at the finish line. Have all of the other players line up at the starting line. The starter shouts "On your mark, get set . . . ." The players prepare by spreading their feet apart, bending over, and grabbing their ankles. Then the starter yells "GO!" and the players race toward the finish line, keeping their legs straight (without bending their knees). Any player who loses the straight leg position must return to the starting line and start over. This game can also be played as a relay race.

Lemonade

Equipment:
- none

Where to Play:

outdoors

Number of Players:

six or more

Directions:

Divide the players into two teams and have them line up along the opposite sides of a playing area that has been clearly defined. Choose one team to go first. The members of this team form a huddle and secretly pick two things: where they want to be from (for example, a city, state, or country) and some action that they want to perform (for example, washing a car, playing a sport, or vacuuming). Then the team moves to the center of the playing area and says "Here we come." The other team asks "From where?" The first team answers with the location that they chose. Then the second team asks "What's your trade?" to which the first team answers "Lemonade!" After saying this they begin to perform the action they decided on earlier. The other team tries to identify the activity by yelling out guesses. When the activity is correctly guessed, a game of tag begins. The acting team runs back to its home line, and the other team tries to catch the team members. After both teams have had an opportunity to perform an action, the team that has tagged the most players is declared the winner.

© Teacher Created Materials, Inc.

Classic Relay Race

Equipment:
  • a baton (or a similar object for passing)

Where to Play:
outdoors, an open area

Number of Players:
six or more

Directions:
Set a start line and a finish line. Divide the players into teams with an equal number of runners in each team. Spread the teams along the race course. For example, on a 100-yard (90m) course with four runners in each team, place the runners 25 yards (23m) apart, beginning at the start line. After a starting signal is given, the first runner in each team, clutching the baton, runs to the second runner and gives him or her the baton. The second runner runs and passes it off to the third, who runs and hands it to the fourth runner. The fourth runner then sprints for the finish line. The first team to have a member cross the finish line wins. If a baton is dropped at any point, that team is disqualified.

Start   Finish

X	X	X	X
X	X	X	X
X	X	X	X
X	X	X	X
X	X	X	X

Gossip Relay

Equipment:
- none

Where to Play:

outdoors

Number of Players:

six or more

Directions:

This game is similar to a classic relay race, but instead of a baton, a phrase is passed from one runner to the next. Before the race begins, the person in charge whispers a phrase to the first runner on each team. The runner runs to the next player and repeats the phrase, and so on. The first team to reach the finish line and repeat the phrase correctly wins.

Crab Relay

Equipment:
- none

Where to Play:

outdoors

Number of Players:

six or more

Directions:

In this relay race, the runners crawl backward on all fours, "crab style," beginning at the start line. When a player reaches the finish line, he or she runs back to the start line and tags the next "crab," who repeats the action. The first team to have all of its players return to the start line wins.

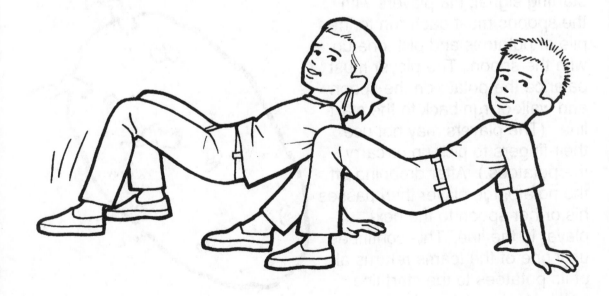

Potato Relay

Equipment:
- small potatoes, one for each player
- plastic spoons

Where to Play:
a large, open area

Number of Players:
four or more

Directions:
Divide the players into two equal teams. Have the teams form two lines behind the start line. Place a pile of potatoes, one for each player, at a line opposite the start line. Give the first runner in each line a plastic spoon. At the starting signal, the players with the spoons must each run to the pile of potatoes and pick one up with the spoon. The player must balance the potato on the spoon and walk or run back to the start line. (The players may not use their fingers to pick up or carry the potatoes.) After dropping off the potato, the player then passes his or her spoon to the next player in the line. This continues until one of the teams returns all of its potatoes to the start line and is declared the winner.

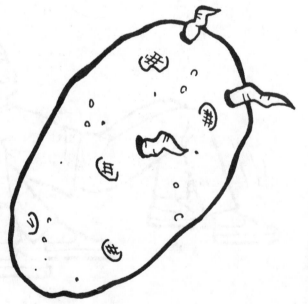

Suitcase Relay

Equipment:
- one suitcase or shopping bag for each team
- clothing—old pajamas, shirts, socks, etc.

Where to Play:
a large, open area

Number of Players:
six or more

Directions:
Before playing, pack each suitcase or bag with an equal number of objects. It is important to keep the items similar as well. Be sure the clothing is large enough to fit over the clothes of every player. Form two or more teams of equal size. Divide the teams in half, and have one group for each team line up at the start line with the other group at the finish line approximately 20–30 yards (18–27 m) away. To begin, have the first player of each team open the suitcase and put on all of the items inside of it. Next, he or she carries the empty suitcase to the other side and removes the clothing, which the waiting player packs back into the suitcase. Then the waiting player takes the suitcase and runs back to the start line. This continues until every player has had a chance to be both the person who puts on the clothes and the person who packs the suitcase. The first team to have all of its players finish both tasks wins.

Pass and Catch

Equipment:
- two balls

Where to Play:

outdoors

Number of Players:

six or more

Directions:

Divide the class into two teams, and choose one player on each team to be its captain. The captains stand behind the throwing line while the rest of their teams stand in lines directly across from them behind the receiving line. The receiving line and the throwing line should be approximately 15 or 20 feet (4.5 or 6 m) apart. After hearing the signal, the captains throw the balls to the first players in the lines. Once the first player of each team catches the ball, he or she runs to the throwing line. The captain of that team then runs to the back of the receiving line. Play continues until a captain receives his or her turn to catch the ball and returns to the throwing line. The team whose captain is the first to return to the throwing line is the winner.

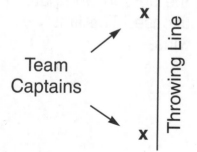

Carry and Fetch Relay

Equipment:
- two beanbags
- chalk

Where to Play:

outdoors

Number of Players:

six or more

Directions:

Divide the players into two teams, and have the teams form two lines. Draw a chalk circle on the ground in front of each line. Give the first player in each team a beanbag. Upon the signal, the first player of each team carries the beanbag and places it inside the team circle. He or she then runs back and tags the hand of the second player who runs to the circle, retrieves the beanbag, and runs back to the line to hand it off to the third player. This pattern continues until all of the players on a team have made the run and are in their original positions. The first team to do so is declared the winner.

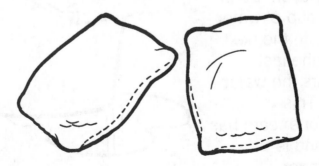

Water Relay

Equipment:
- two pails of water
- two paper cups
- two milk bottles

Where to Play:

outdoors

Number of Players:

six or more

Directions:

Divide the players into two teams and have the teams form two lines. Place a pail of water at one end of each line and an empty bottle at the other end of each line. Give empty paper cups to the players next to the pails. At the sound of the starting signal, the players with the cups should scoop up a cupful of water and pass it on to the next player. Each team passes a cup of water from one player to the next until it reaches the last player who pours the water into the bottle. This continues until one team has filled its bottle and is declared the winner.

78

© Teacher Created Materials, Inc.

Circle Passing Relay

Equipment:
- two beanbags or balls

Where to Play:

outside or any large area

Number of Players:

10 or more players per team

Directions:

Divide the players into two teams, and have them form two circles. Choose one person in each team to be the captain. At the starting signal the captain begins passing the beanbag around the circle to the right. When it gets back to the captain, he or she calls out "One" and continues passing it. When the beanbag has made another rotation, the captain calls out "Two." When the captain receives the bag for the third time, the team members raise their hands to indicate that they have finished. The first team members to raise their hands are declared the winners.

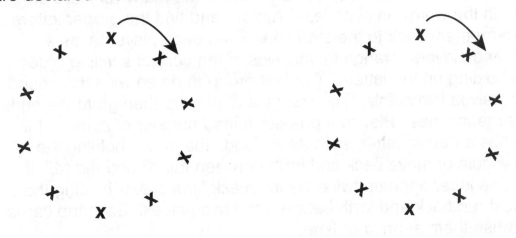

Alphabet Scramble

Equipment:
- white index cards
- colored index cards
- a marker
- two chairs

Where to Play:

indoors

Number of Players:

8 to 20

Directions:

Prior to playing this game, prepare two sets of alphabet cards on white and colored index cards. Use a marker to write one letter on each card. Place the card sets on two chairs which are placed about 10 feet (3 m) from a start line. Divide the players into two equal teams and have the teams line up behind the start line. When the leader calls out a word, the first few players (as many as there are letters in the word) on each team run out and find the proper letters and carry them back to the start line. Then each player takes a letter, and players arrange themselves in the correct spelling order while holding up the letters. The first group to do so wins that round and receives five points. The first sets of players then go to the ends of their team lines. Play to a predetermined number of points. If the word has a double letter, such as in "food," the player holding the "o" must wiggle or move back and forth between the "f" and the "d." If the same letter appears twice, as in "check," the player holding the "c" must run back and forth between the two places. Save the cards and reuse them at another time.

© *Teacher Created Materials, Inc.*

Chopstick-Balloon Relay

Equipment:
- two balloons
- four sets of chopsticks
- two cones

Where to Play:

indoors or outdoors

Number of Players:

six or more

Directions:

Divide the players into two teams, and line them up single file. Place a cone across from each line. Give sets of chopsticks to the first two people of each team. The first player of each team holds a balloon between his or her chopsticks. At the starting signal, the first player runs around the cone and returns to hand off the balloon to the second player, using only the chopsticks. The first player then gives the chopsticks to the third player while the second player runs off to make a lap around the cone. If a balloon is dropped, it can only be picked up by using the chopsticks. The play continues until every player has had the opportunity to make a lap around the cone. The first team to get all of its players back in line is the winner.

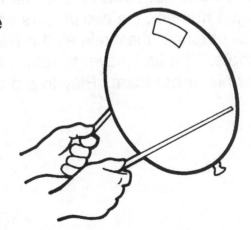

Leapfrog Relay

Equipment:
- none

Where to Play:

indoors or outdoors

Number of Players:

8 to 14

Directions:

Arrange the players in a circle facing counterclockwise. Divide the circle in half to create two teams and then number the players on each team. Assign the players numbers so that each player has someone with the same number directly across from him or her. (For example, if there are 12 players, number half the circle 1–6 and then also number the other half of the circle 1–6. The ones should be across from each other, as should be the twos, threes, etc.) Ask the players to get down on their hands and knees. When the leader calls out a number, the two players with that number have to leapfrog over the others in the circle all the way around and back to their original spots. The first player to return to the correct position wins a point for his or her team. Play to a predetermined number of points.

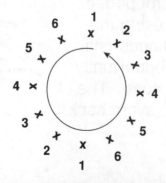

82

© Teacher Created Materials, Inc.

Run, Toss, Catch Relay

Equipment:
- a net or rope stretched between two posts and 8 feet (2.4 m) off of the ground
- a baseline marked 30 feet (9 m) from, and parallel to, the net
- volleyballs, utility balls, softballs, or beanbags.

Where to Play:
a large, open space

Number of Players:
4 to 40

Directions:
Divide the players into two or more teams, and have them form single file lines behind the baseline, facing the net. Designate the first person in each line to be the captain, and give him or her a ball. At the sound of the start signal, the captain of each team runs to the net, throws the ball over it, catches it, and runs back to hand it off to the next player standing behind the baseline. The captain then goes to the end of the line while the next player does the same exercise. If a player misses or drops the ball after throwing it over the net, he or she must continue until it is caught. The first team to have all of their players finish is the winner.

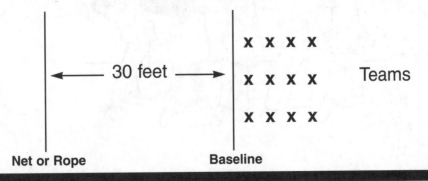

Choo-Choo Relay

Equipment:
- none

Where to Play:

any area approximately 25 feet (7.6 m) in length

Number of Players:

eight or more

Directions:

Divide the players into two lines, and have each player pick a partner from within the line. When the partners move in this relay, they move together as two cars of a train. One person stands behind the other and holds onto his or her partner's hips. Then they shuffle along without lifting their feet. At the signal to start, the first set of partners from each team goes to a designated turning point about 25 feet (7.6 m) away, switches positions, and heads back to the starting line where they tag the next pair who do the same thing. The first team to have all of its pairs complete the activity wins.

Newspaper Race

Equipment:
- two newspaper sheets per player

Where to Play:

indoors or outdoors

Number of Players:

four or more

Directions:

Divide the players into two teams, and have them line up behind the start line. Give each player two sheets of newspaper. The first players leave the start line, race to a predetermined turning point, and return to the start line. While they are racing they may only move by stepping on their pieces of newspaper. A player may step on one paper, lay the other one down and step on it, pick up the one he or she just stepped off of and drop it down for the next step, etc. The first team to get all of their players back across the starting line is the winner.

Bear Race

Equipment:
- none

Where to Play:
anywhere

Number of Players:
any number

Directions:

Before beginning this game, have the players practice walking like bears. To walk like a bear, a person must put his or her hands on the ground and move the left hand and the right foot forward at the same time. Then the right hand and the left foot are moved forward together. When the players have had enough practice at this, mark a start line on the ground and a finish line about 20 feet (6 m) away.

Line up teams of four behind the start line. At the starting signal, the first player on each team walks like a bear to the finish line. The next player follows until all of the team members have crossed the finish line. The first team to complete the race wins.

Obstacle Course Kickball

Equipment:
- two different colors of rubber balls, to fit inside coffee cans
- boards and bricks to create ramps
- cardboard boxes, rocks, and other objects to create obstacles
- three or more coffee cans, opened on both ends and taped together to form a tunnel
- chalk, masking tape, or pebbles
- scissors

Where to Play:

a large, open area

Number of Players:

four or more

Directions:

Determine the start and the finish lines, and mark them with chalk, tape, or pebbles. As a group, work together to create an obstacle course, including ramps, tunnels, cutouts from cardboard, chairs, etc., which the players will kick the balls through. Divide the players into teams of no fewer than two and no more than six players each. Explain the rules of the course, and choose someone to act as a referee. At the referee's signal, the first kicker on each team kicks the ball as far as possible along the course. The team members run after their balls, kicking them along, and making sure to keep their balls as close to the route as possible. No team member may kick the ball more than twice in a row. Team members may not kick their opponent's ball away from the course. The first team to kick the ball across the finish line wins the game.

Cotton Ball Race

Equipment:
- one large cotton ball for each player
- masking tape

Where to Play:

on a floor

Number of Players:

two or more

Directions:

Place one long piece of masking tape on the floor to mark a start line and another piece to mark a finish line. Position two to four players on their hands and knees at the start line. In front of each player, place a cotton ball. Instruct the racers that when a signal is given, they are to begin blowing upon their cotton balls. The first person to get his or her cotton ball across the finish line is the winner.

88

© *Teacher Created Materials, Inc.*

One-Pitch Softball

Equipment:
- a softball
- bases

Where to Play:

a softball field or an open area

Number of Players:

eight or more

Directions:

This game is similar to traditional softball. However, the differences are that each team uses its own pitcher and that each player is thrown only one pitch. If the pitch is missed, fouled, caught, or not swung at, it is an out. Each player is given a turn at bat, but the bases are cleared each time three outs are accrued.

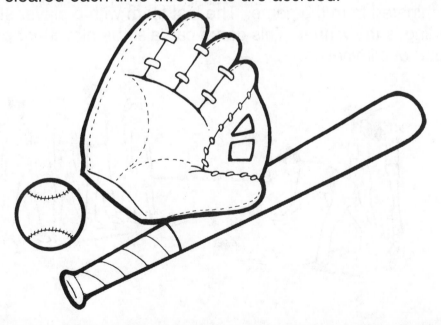

Brooklyn Bridge

Equipment:
- a ball

Where to Play:

a paved area

Number of Players:

six or more

Directions:

Divide the players into two teams, and line up the teams, facing each other about 15 feet (4.5 m) apart. The players should stand with their feet spread apart far enough to allow a ball to pass through. The teams take turns at trying to roll the ball through the legs of the opposing players. The players are not allowed to move or to try to stop the ball. If the ball passes through someone's legs, that person is eliminated from the game. The last team with a player still standing is the winner. This game can also be played for points instead of elimination.

Ball Punch

Equipment:
- a large rubber ball

Where to Play:

outdoors

Number of Players:

at least eight

Directions:

Designate one player to be "it." Have the rest of the players form a large circle by standing three to four feet (.9–1.2 m) apart and facing inward. "It" stands outside of the circle. One player begins by handing the ball in either direction. Each player has the choice of handing the ball to the left or right, but the ball cannot be passed across the circle or skip anyone. As the ball is being passed, "it" tries to punch it into the middle of the circle. When "it" succeeds in punching the ball into the circle, the last person to touch the ball is then the new "it."

Newcomb

Equipment:
- a volleyball or utility ball
- a rope or net

Where to Play:

outdoors

Number of Players:

eight or more

Directions:

Newcomb is similar to volleyball. The ball is thrown and caught, not hit as in volleyball. Set up a similar court area, but take into consideration the players' ages and available space. Divide the players into two teams, and place them on opposite sides of the net or rope. Flip a coin to see which team will go first. Any player from the first team throws the ball over the net, hoping it will hit the ground before it is caught. If it does, the serving team scores a point. If it is caught, the ball remains in play until it finally falls to the ground. If it falls on the serving team's side, the next serve goes to the other side. If the ball hits the net, goes under the net, or goes out of bounds without anyone touching it, the other team gets to serve. The first team to score at least 21 points and lead by at least two points is the winner.

92

© Teacher Created Materials, Inc.

Horse

Equipment:
- a basketball or utility ball
- a basketball hoop

Where to Play:

outdoors or in a gymnasium

Number of Players:

no more than five per hoop

Directions:

Divide the players into groups of five or fewer and have them count off to determine the order of play. The first player in a group takes the basketball and attempts a shot from anywhere in a predetermined playing area. (For younger players make the area smaller.) If the shot is made, the second player then has to make the same shot from wherever and however the first player took it. If the second player misses, he or she is given the letter "H." If the second player makes the same shot, play continues until someone misses or until play comes around again to the person who took the initial shot. If the initial shooter misses a shot, the second player then has the opportunity to take a shot from wherever he or she wishes. Encourage the players to be creative with their shots, for example, standing backwards or with their eyes closed. When a player earns all of the letters in "HORSE," he or she is out of the game. The last player in the game is the winner.

Touch Football

Equipment:
- a football

Where to Play:

outdoors

Number of Players:

at least four people for each team

Directions:

Mark off the area that you want to designate as the playing field, keeping in mind the ages, sizes, and skill levels of your players. For younger, less skilled players, make the field smaller so that it will be easier for them to score. In touch football you can be very flexible with the rules. Normally, the offense gets four tries to move the ball 10 yards. However, if playing on a shortened field, you can amend these rules so that the team gets four tries to get to the halfway point of the field or, on a very shortened field, four tries to score a touchdown. Begin play by flipping a coin to see who receives or kicks off. The kickoff can either be kicked or passed. The receiver tries to catch and carry the ball as close as possible to the other team's goal line without being touched by both hands of an opposing player. Play stops whenever the ball carrier is touched with both hands by an opponent. Have the offensive team line up in a huddle before each play to outline some type of play to run.

Touch Football *(cont.)*

If the players have the ability to throw the football, have them try some pass receiving patterns. You can have the offensive players rotate positions so that everyone gets a chance to be the quarterback. You may want to have the defensive players count to five before beginning their rush so that the play can have some time to develop, but because there are no hard and fast rules, be ready to add or amend rules as the game progresses. When a player crosses the other team's goal line, it is a touchdown and the player's team scores seven points. Extra points and field goals are not used in touch football. After a team scores it lines up on its own side of the field and kicks off to the opposing team. Play for a predetermined length of time. The team who is ahead at the end of the decided time is considered the winner.

Home Plate Baseball

Equipment:
- a tennis ball
- bases

Where to Play:

outdoors

Number of Players:

six or more

Directions:

Divide the players into two equal teams and decide who will bat first. Designate the playing field as a small diamond (each side should be about 10 feet or 3 m) with a pitcher's mound about five feet (1.5 m) from home plate. To begin play, one player from the pitching team stands on the mound while another stands behind home plate as the catcher. A player from the hitting team steps up to home plate as the hitter. Everyone else stands on the sidelines. The pitcher tosses the ball (underhanded) towards home plate, and the hitter tries to hit it with his or her hand onto the field. If the ball is hit, the hitter runs and tries to get to first base before the pitcher can retrieve the ball and run in to touch home plate. If the pitcher succeeds, the runner is out. Before pitching begins again, the players rotate positions. The catcher becomes the pitcher, a new player from the pitching team comes in to be the catcher, and the old pitcher goes to the sidelines. The play continues as in regular baseball, with each team getting three outs before switching sides. Play for a predetermined number of innings. The team with the most runs at the end of the game wins.

© Teacher Created Materials, Inc.

Kickball

Equipment:
- a utility ball or a volleyball
- bases

Where to Play:

outdoors

Number of Players:

at least five players for each team

Directions:

Kickball is a simplified version of baseball. Divide the players into two teams, and decide who will be the first team to kick. Spread the players evenly throughout the playing area. Ideally, you would have nine players on each side, positioned as in baseball, but this is not absolutely necessary. To begin playing, the pitcher rolls the ball to home plate and a player from the kicking team tries to kick it. Foul kicks are counted as strikes, but you can never get a third strike on a foul. If the ball is kicked into fair territory, the runner can be called "out" in one of four ways: (1) if the ball is kicked into the air and caught, (2) if the ball is fielded and thrown to the first baseman before the runner gets to first base, (3) if the runner is tagged with the ball, or (4) if the runner is tagged below the waist by a thrown ball. If the runner is hit above the waist, he or she is still safe. Play continues as in baseball, with the sides changing after three outs. If there is a shortage of players, you can elect someone on the batting team to be catcher with only the responsibility of returning the ball after the pitches. In this case, the pitcher would cover home plate for his or her team once the ball is in play. The team that is leading after a predetermined number of innings is declared the winner.

Battle Ball

Equipment:
- a utility ball

Where to Play:
outside

Number of Players:
10 or more

Directions:
Mark off a square playing area appropriate for the number of people playing and put the ball in the middle. Choose one player to be the referee, and divide the rest into two teams. Assign each player on each team a number. The teams line up numerically on opposite sides of the square. The referee begins the game by calling out a number, and the two players (one from each team) who have that number sprint for the ball in the center. The first player to get the ball remains in the center while the other roams around the square. The player in the middle tries to tag the other player with the ball. If the player at whom the ball is thrown catches it, a point is scored for his or her team. If the thrown ball misses the player, no point is scored. If the ball bounces before touching the player at whom it is thrown, that player can throw it back if he or she can gain control of it before it goes out of bounds. Play continues until the referee calls out a new number. The first team to score 21 points is the winner.

Running Bases

Equipment:
- two bases
- a ball

Where to Play:

outdoors

Number of Players:

three

Directions:

Two players serve as fielders, and the third player is the base runner. The fielders stand next to the bases. If bases are not available, they can be drawn with chalk or marked with sticks. The bases should be placed between 30 and 50 feet (9 and 15 m) apart, depending upon the players' abilities. To start the game, the runner stands on one base with a fielder. The other fielder throws the ball, and the runner sprints to the opposite base. As the runner runs, the fielders try to tag him or her. This often results in a "pickle," with the fielders throwing the ball back and forth until the runner safely tags the base or they tag the runner. If a runner is tagged, he or she must trade places with the tagger. If the players wish to keep score, they can count each time a runner makes it safely to a base as a hit. Four hits equal one run.

Octopus Ball

Equipment:
- a playground ball or a volleyball

Where to Play:
a large, grassy area

Number of Players:
10 to 30

Directions:
Set up a playing area that is approximately 100 feet (30.4 m) long and 50 to 70 feet (15.2 to 21.3 m) wide. Select one player to be "it." Line up the rest of the players at one end of the playing field. On the signal from "it," all of the runners attempt to run to the other end of the field. "It" attempts to hit any of the participants below the waist with the ball. When a runner is hit, he or she must sit down in the place where he or she was tagged. The tagged player then becomes part of the "it" team and attempts to tag the runners. The tagged players must remain sitting. When a runner is tagged by one of the sitting players, he or she must sit down and also try to tag the other runners. Only "it" can throw the ball and move around the field. The last runner to be tagged becomes "it" for the next game. If a runner goes out of bounds, he or she must sit and become one of the players who tags.

Washington Square

Equipment:
- a playground ball or volleyball

Where to Play:
a large, open area

Number of Players:
six or more

Directions:
Have the players form a circle with everyone facing toward the center. All of the participants should stand with their legs spread shoulder-width apart. Each player's feet should be touching the feet of the player next to him or her. Begin the game by tossing the ball into the circle. The object of the game is to hit, throw, kick, or roll the ball through another player's legs. If the ball passes through a player's legs, he or she is eliminated, and the circle becomes smaller. Play continues until there is only one player remaining.

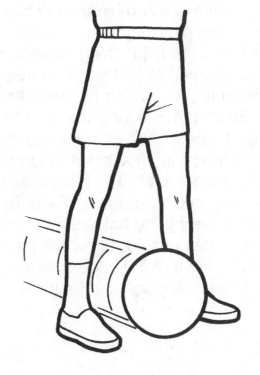

German Bat Ball

Equipment:
- a volleyball or playground ball
- a home plate
- one base

Where to Play:

outdoors

Number of Players:

10 or more

Directions:

This game is a combination of baseball, volleyball, and dodge ball. Divide the players into two teams. The hitter throws the ball up and hits it into the field, using either a hand or fist. The ball must go over a line marked at 10 feet (3 m) away to be a fair hit. There are no strikeouts. After a fair hit, the hitter runs to the base which is placed 15–30 feet (4.5–9.1 m) from the home plate. Then the hitter runs back to home plate. Meanwhile, the fielders try to field the ball and then throw it in an attempt to tag the hitter before he or she can reach home plate. The hitter may try to avoid being hit by ducking, dodging, and zigzagging. Fielders are allowed to take only one step after retrieving the ball and can hold it for only five seconds before he or she must pass or throw the ball at the hitter. A player is out if a fly ball is caught or if he/she is tagged. There are three outs per team, per inning. A game can be played for seven or nine innings.

© *Teacher Created Materials, Inc.*

Rocket Launch and Recovery

Equipment:
- a five to six foot (1.5 to 1.8 m) canvas square
- a utility ball

Where to Play:

outdoors

Number of Players:

8 to 18

Directions:

Have four players hold the corners of the canvas square and catapult the ball into the air. The other players try to catch the ball after it is launched. The four launchers launch the ball by extending their arms and then giving the cloth a sudden jerk. With a little practice they can launch the ball with surprising speed and at various angles. After one of the catchers has caught the ball three times (not necessarily in a row), he or she replaces one of the launchers.

Blizzard

Equipment:
- a Ping-Pong ball
- newspapers

Where to Play:

indoors or outdoors

Number of Players:

10

Directions:

Divide the players into two teams of five. Mark off a playing area with a goal line at each end. Have each player make a fan out of the newspaper. Place the Ping-Pong ball in the center of the playing area. Each team then tries to fan the ball towards the other team's goal without ever letting the fan touch the ball. If a team gets the ball across their opponent's goal line, they score a point. Play can continue for a predetermined length of time or up to a certain number of points.

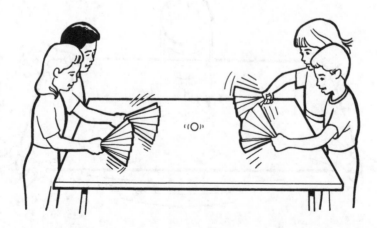

104

© *Teacher Created Materials, Inc.*

Evasion Ball

Equipment:
   • a volleyball

Where to Play:
a large, open area

Number of Players:
15 or more

Directions:
Divide the players into three equal teams. Teams 1 and 2 form the two sidelines, facing each other about 25 feet (7.6 meters) apart. Team 3 is the running team and is lined up in the middle. Consecutively number the players of Team 3. To begin playing, throw the volleyball to Team 1. Player number one on the running team (Team 3) immediately starts running between the two side teams, around the goal, and back to the starting point. A run is scored if he or she is not hit by the ball. If player number one is hit, he or she is out, and player number two starts to run. (**Note:** A player can only be hit below the shoulders. If a runner is hit above the shoulders, the player who threw the ball is out.) When the entire team has had a turn, their score is added up. Team 3 then replaces Team 1, Team 1 replaces Team 2, and Team 2 becomes the running team.

Goal

X	X	X
X	X	X
X	X	X
X	X	X
X	X	X

Team 1   Team 2

Team 3

Human Pinball

Equipment:
- a utility ball or a volleyball

Where to Play:

outdoors

Number of Players:

six or more

Directions:

Choose one person to be the target. Have the rest of the players stand in a circle, facing outward. They should stand with their feet spread apart and touching the feet of the people on either side of them. Have them bend down, swinging their arms between their legs. These represent the pinball flippers. Have the one player that was chosen earlier stand inside of the circle. The flippers then try to hit the player with the ball, using only their hands as paddles. The player in the middle tries to avoid the ball for as long as possible. The human flipper who manages to hit the player in the middle then becomes the new target.

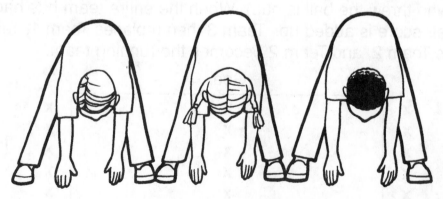

Four Square

Equipment:
- a utility ball or a volleyball
- chalk

Where to Play:

a paved area

Number of Players:

four or more

Directions:

On the pavement, draw a 16 x 16 feet (4.8 x 4.8 m) square (smaller if the players are young), and divide it into four equal squares. Label the squares A, B, C, and D, and place one player in each square. If there are more than four players, the extra players stand in line outside of the square and wait for their turns. The player in square D starts by bouncing the ball once and swatting it into one of the other squares. The receiver allows the ball to bounce once before hitting it into another square. A player who misses or fails to return the ball must move to area D, and the other players move up. If player D commits an error, he or she is out of the game, and the first person in line moves into square D. The four ways of committing fouls are (1) failure to return the ball to another square, (2) striking the ball with a fist, (3) causing the ball to land on a line, and (4) allowing the ball to touch any part of the body except the hands. The object of the game is to advance to area A and stay there for as long as possible.

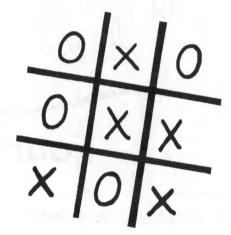

Rainy-Day Games

Beetle

Equipment:
- one die
- paper
- pencils

Where to Play:

at a table

Number of Players:

two to six

Directions:

The object of this game is to be the player to complete the drawing of a "beetle." The players determine their order by rolling the die. The player to roll the highest number goes first. The first player tries to roll the number one. If this player is not successful, he or she passes the die to the next player. Each player gets one roll per turn. The numbers must be rolled in order from one to five. When a player rolls a one, he or she draws the body of the beetle. The head is drawn when any player rolls a two. The number three must be rolled twice—once to draw three legs on one side of the body and again to draw the three legs on the other side of the body. The number four must be rolled twice also. The first four allows a player to draw one antenna, and the second four is needed for the other antenna. A player can draw one eye after rolling a five. The first player to roll a second five can add the other eye. This completes the beetle, and the final player wins the game.

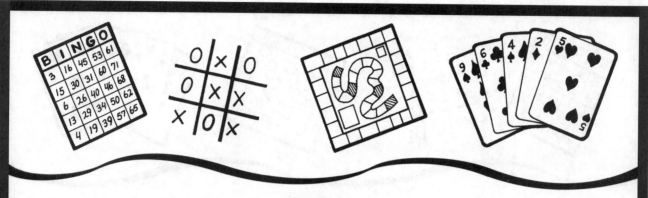

I Spy

Equipment:
- none

Where to Play:

anywhere

Number of Players:

four or more

Directions:

The object of this game is to guess the object spied by another player. One player begins the game by mentally choosing an object in the room. He or she says "I spy something beginning with the letter b." (The person in this example has spied an object beginning with the letter "b.") In no particular order, the other players offer their guesses. The spy lets them know if they are correct.

> **Player:** "Ball?"
> **Spy:** "No."
> **Player:** "Book?"
> **Spy:** "No."
> **Player:** "Blackboard?"
> **Spy:** "Yes."

The next spy is the player who guesses correctly.

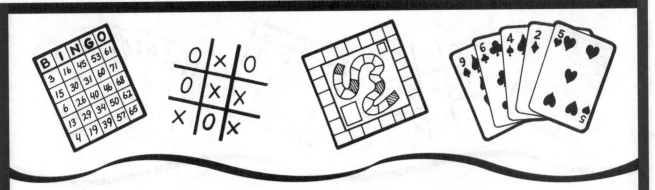

Twenty Questions

Equipment:
- none

Where to Play:

anywhere

Number of Players:

three or more

Directions:

In this game, it is the player's goal to guess the object chosen by another player by asking questions. One player thinks of an object and then tells the group whether it is an animal, vegetable, or mineral. One by one the rest of the players ask questions about the object. The questions must require a yes or no answer and should be aimed at helping to discover the identity of the object. The players get 20 chances to ask questions. If a player guesses incorrectly before all 20 questions have been asked, he or she is eliminated (this guess does not count as a question). If the object is revealed after twenty questions, the player who first thought of the object wins the game.

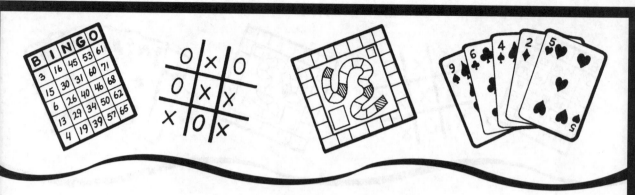

Hot and Cold

Equipment:

- an object that can be easily hidden

Where to Play:

in a room where an object can be hidden

Number of players:

four or more

Directions:

Choose one player to be the searcher for the first round. He or she leaves the room, and the remaining players hide an object. After the searcher is brought back into the room, he or she begins looking for the object. If the player is far away from the object, the other players say "cold." If the player gets near the object they say "warm," then "hot," and, finally, "burning" when the player has almost found the object. The game is over when the object is found.

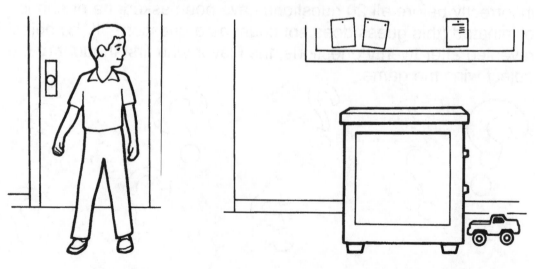

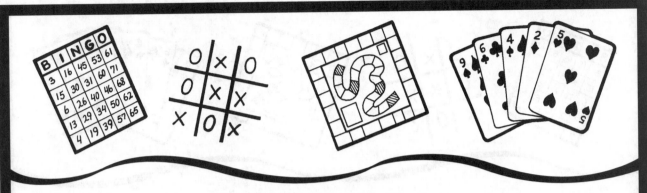

Hunt the Key

Equipment:
- a small object that can be held in the hand

Where to Play:

anywhere

Number of Players:

eight or more

Directions:

The object of this game is for the hunter to figure out who has the "key" and for the other players to hide the location of the "key" from the hunter. The players sit closely together in a circle. The hunter sits in the center of the circle. The hunter closes his or her eyes, and a small object is given to one of the players. The players pass and/or pretend to pass the object to each other without showing it. The hunter watches and tries to guess who has the object. When the hunter thinks he or she knows who has the "key," he or she says the name of the player. The player must reveal whether he or she has the key. That player becomes the hunter if he or she does have the "key." If the hunter guesses incorrectly, the game continues.

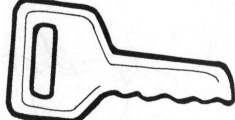

My Grandma Owns a Grocery Store

Equipment:
- none

Where to Play:

anywhere

Number of Players:

four or more

Directions:

The first player says "My grandma owns a grocery store and she sells apples." The next player says "My grandma owns a grocery store, and she sells apples and pickles." The game continues with each player adding an item until a player cannot list the items in the correct order. The player is eliminated, and the game continues. The last remaining player is the winner. You may want to have the players choose items in alphabetical order (for example, . . .apples, . . . beef, . . . cookies) to make it easier for them to remember the objects.

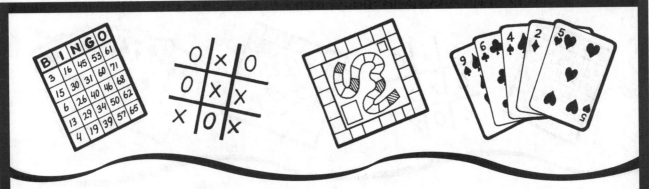

Memory Game

Equipment:
- an assortment of 25 small objects
- a tray
- a towel
- paper
- pencils

Where to Play:

anywhere

Number of Players:

two or more

Directions:

Before the game begins, randomly arrange the objects on the tray. Gently cover the tray with the towel. Place the tray where all of the players can see it well. Remove the towel from the tray for about a minute while the players try to memorize what objects are on the tray. Cover the tray again. Ask the players to try to write down as many objects as they can remember. Give them a specified amount of time to make their lists. The player with the most complete list is the winner.

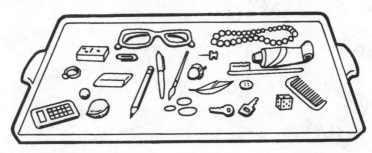

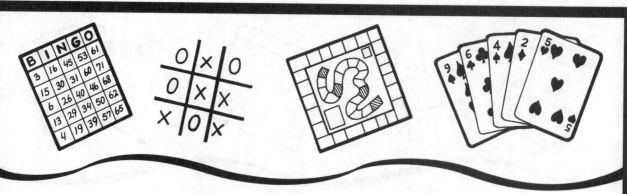

Spelling Chain

Equipment:
- a list of words appropriate for the ages of the participants

Where to Play:
anywhere

Number of Players:
two or more

Directions:
Choose one person to serve as the spelling master (preferably an adult or mature child). The spelling master asks the first player to spell a word. If it is spelled correctly, the child receives a point. If it is spelled incorrectly, it is the next player's turn, and he or she is given a new word to spell. The player with the most points wins the game. A time limit for the game should be agreed upon before the game begins.

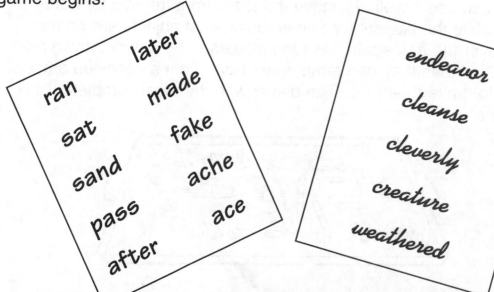

Ha, Ha, Ha

Equipment:
- none

Where to Play:

anywhere

Number of Players:

two or more

Directions:

The object of this game is not to laugh. Have the players form a circle. The first player begins by saying "Ha"; the next player says "Ha, Ha." Each player adds another "Ha." Any player who starts laughing must drop out of the circle. However, he or she can continue to try to make the others laugh by doing anything except touching the other players. The most serious player wins the game.

HA, HA

HA, HA

HA, HA

HA, HA

HA, HA

HA, HA

HA, HA

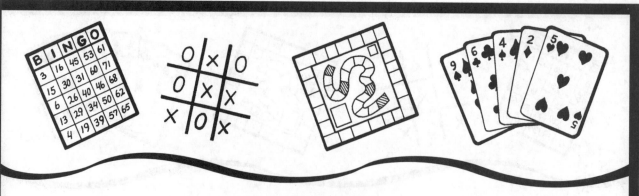

Animals

Equipment:
- a deck of playing cards

Where to Play:

at a table

Number of Players:

three to ten

Directions:

In this game the object is to win another player's cards by calling out his or her animal noise before he or she calls out yours. Shuffle the cards and deal them out, facedown. Each player chooses an animal to imitate. (Go around the circle a couple of times to practice the animal sounds.) One player might baa like a sheep, another neigh like a horse, another tweet like a bird, yet another croak like a frog, etc. Each player needs to remember the animals chosen by the other players. Play begins at the dealer's left. Everyone around the table discards one card, faceup. Each player forms a separate discard pile. When one player lays down a card that is of equal value to another card in someone else's discard pile (two queens, for instance), the players with the matching cards quickly try to call out the animal noise of the other. For example, if a "horse" and a "sheep" both discard a queen, the "horse" baas and the "sheep" neighs. The first of the two players to make the right sound gets the discard pile of the other player. A player who makes an incorrect noise or calls out a noise at the incorrect time must give up the top card of his or her discard pile. Players who lose all their cards are eliminated from the game. The player to collect all of the cards is the winner.

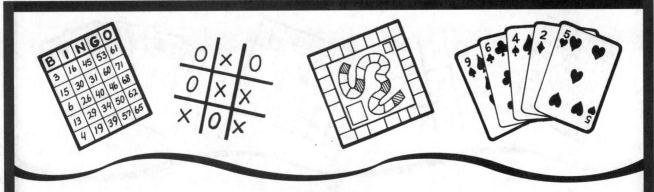

Bango

Equipment:

- a deck of playing cards

Where to Play:

at a table

Number of Players:

three to five

Directions:

This game is a simplified version of Bingo. It is a great game for children under eight. A player shuffles the cards and deals five cards to each player. The players place their cards faceup in front of them. The dealer then turns the remaining cards over one at a time, calling out the value (not the suit) of each card. Any player with a card of matching value can turn that card facedown. The first player to turn all five cards facedown yells "Bango!" and wins the round. A grand winner is determined by keeping track of how many rounds are won by each player.

Crazy Eights

Equipment:
- a deck of playing cards

Where to Play:

at a table

Number of players:

three to five

Directions:

The dealer shuffles the cards and deals seven to each player. The dealer then places the remaining cards in a pile in the center of the table. The players examine and sort their cards, keeping them hidden from their opponents. The player at the dealer's left starts the game by laying one card faceup in the center of the table. The next player must follow with a card of the same suit—a heart on a heart, for example. If a player does not have a card of the same suit, or wants to change the suit, a card of the same value may be laid down. For example, a seven may be played on a seven, which then changes the suit to the one on the face of the card. Eights are "wild," meaning that they can be played at any time. The player using an eight gets to choose the suit for the next player to follow. When a player is not able to use the same suit, rank, or an eight, he or she must draw from the center pile. If the card drawn can be played, it is laid down. If not, the player must continue to draw until he or she draws a card that can be played. The first player to discard all of his or her cards is the winner.

Donkey

Equipment:
- a deck of playing cards

Where to Play:

at a table

Number of Players:

three to eight

Directions:

To begin this game, the dealer should prepare the deck by pulling out sets of four of a kind, the number of sets determined by the number of players. If there are three players, the dealer pulls out three sets of four of a kind. The remaining cards are set aside and not used. The cards are then shuffled and dealt. Each player discreetly examines his or her hand and chooses one card to discard. The object of the game is to have four cards of equal value. If a player is dealt two queens, a two, and a four, the two or four should be discarded. The discarded card is placed facedown on the table. When everyone has discarded one card, each player passes the discarded card to the player on his or her left. The players then pick up the new cards to see if they can be used. If a card can be used, it is added to the player's hand and the player chooses another card to discard. If it cannot be used, it is discarded.

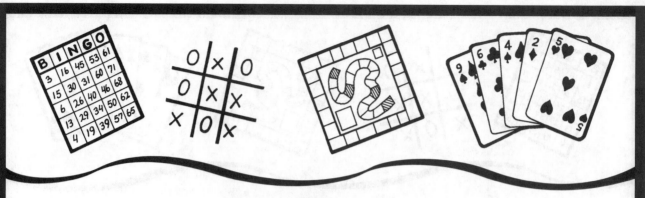

Donkey *(cont.)*

The passing of the cards should be done as quickly as possible. When a player has obtained four matching cards, he or she lays them on the table and places a finger next to his or her nose. When the other players notice that the cards have been put down and the player is using the nose signal, they must hurry to put their fingers next to their noses also. The last player to give the nose signal is the "donkey" of that round. That player is given a "D." After a player has lost six rounds and has been assigned D-O-N-K-E-Y, he or she is declared the loser.

Dress Me

Equipment:
- an old, large shirt

Where to Play:

anywhere

Number of players:

four or more

Directions:

In this game the players try to move a shirt from one player to another while holding hands. One player puts on the shirt and holds the hand of another player. The rest of the players try to take the shirt off of the player wearing it and put it on the other player without breaking the handhold. The only way that this can be done is by turning the shirt inside out as it goes over the head of the first player. Once it is on the next player, another player joins hands with the player now wearing the shirt. The first player becomes a dresser. If there are enough players and shirts, this can be done in teams as a race.

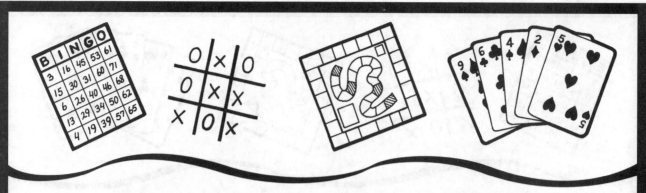

How Do You Do, Shoe?

Equipment:

• the shoes on the players' feet

Where to Play:

anywhere

Number of Players:

eight or more

Directions:

Have the players sit in a circle on the floor, take off their shoes, and place them in front of themselves. When the signal is given, the players pick up their shoes and begin quickly passing them in one direction. When the signal "Change!" is given, the shoes are passed in the other direction. When the signal "Find!" is given, the players try to retrieve their own shoes as they are passed around. The shoes are passed until everyone has his or her own shoes back.

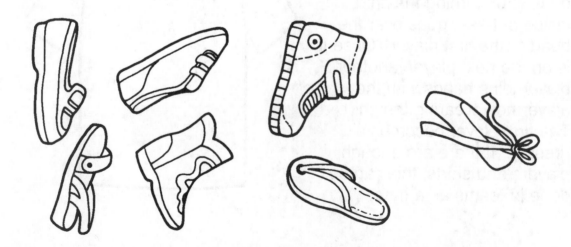

Magazine Scavenger Hunt

Equipment:
- magazines
- list of items
- pencils
- paper

Where to Play:

anywhere

Number of Players:

two or more

Directions:

This game can be played in groups or individually. Each group or individual should have a pencil and paper to keep track of the found items. Prepare a list of items before the game. The list should contain common items and items easily found in magazines. (While making up the list, keep in mind the types of magazines that will be available for the players.) Each group or individual is given 10 or 15 minutes to look through the magazines to search for the listed items. When an item is found, the page number and magazine should be noted on a sheet of paper. If a group finds all of the items before the time runs out, they win. If the time runs out before all of the items are found, the group with the most complete list wins.

List
perfume
clothing
a toy
movie
computer
book
figurine

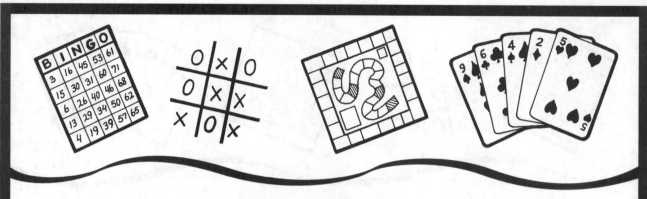

Old Maid

Equipment:
- a deck of cards

Where to Play:

at a table

Number of Players:

three or more

Directions:

Before beginning this game, remove the queen of hearts from the deck. Shuffle the cards and deal the entire deck (excluding the queen) to the players. Each player examines his or her hand, matches any pairs of equal value (two fours, two aces, etc.), and places them facedown on the table. When all of the players have gone through their cards, the player on the left of the dealer pulls one card from the hand of the player immediately to his or her right. If the drawn card can be paired with any of the cards already in the player's hand, the two are removed and laid with any previous pairs, facedown on the table. If not, play resumes with the next player. The next player on the left draws a card from the player on his or her right. Play continues around the circle until one player is left with the odd queen. This player is the "Old Maid" and loses the game.

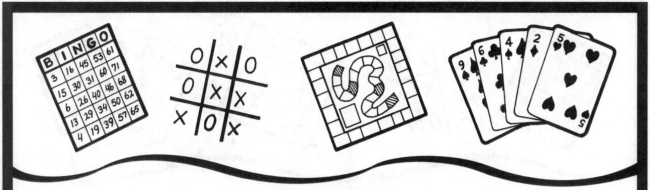

Odd Bean

Equipment:
- 12 dried beans for each player
- small bags to hold the beans

Where to Play:
at a table or on the floor

Number of Players:
two or more

Directions:
Give each player a bag containing 12 beans. A player hides some beans in his or her fist and asks the next player, "Odds or evens?" If the player guesses correctly, he or she gets to keep the beans. If the guess is wrong, the guessing player must give the same number of beans to the player holding the beans. The second player then holds a certain number of beans in his or her hand and asks the third player the same question. When a player loses all of his or her beans he or she must drop out of the game. A time limit can be set. The person with the most beans at the end of this time period is declared the winner.

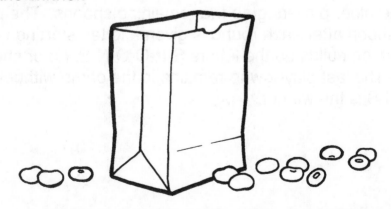

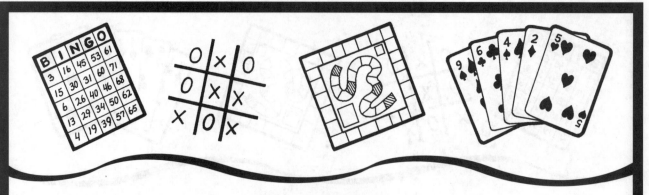

Spoons

Equipment:
- a deck of playing cards
- spoons

Where to Play:

at a table

Number of Players:

three or more

Directions:

Place enough spoons for all of the players except one in the center of the table. Pull out a set of four of a kind from the deck for each player, and set aside the rest of the cards. For example, if there are four players, there should be four sets. Shuffle the sets of cards, and deal them to the players. The goal of each player is to try to get four of a kind. After the players have had a chance to look at their cards, they each discard one. The discarded card is then passed to the left. Each player picks up his or her new card. The cards are examined, and each player discards one and passes it to the left. When a player collects four cards of the same value, he or she grabs for a spoon. The other players grab the remaining spoons. The player left without a spoon after each round is given a letter, starting with S. When a person builds up the letters S-P-O-O-N-S, he or she is out of the game. The last player who remains in the game without spelling S-P-O-O-N-S is the winner.

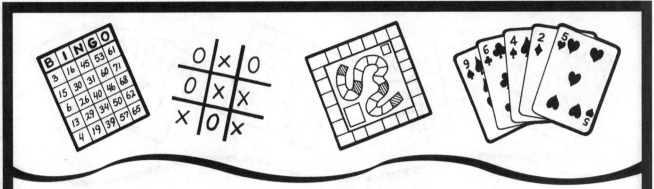

I Doubt It

Equipment:
• playing cards

Where to Play:
at a table

Number of Players:
three or more

Directions:
Shuffle the deck and deal it out to the players. The player on the dealer's left starts the game by laying any card from his or her hand facedown in the center of the table and calling out its value at the same time. The next player's goal is to follow the last card laid down with a card of the next higher value. For example, if the first card laid down was a nine, then the next player wants to lay down a 10. The card is laid facedown, and the player calls out the number 10, regardless of whether this is actually a 10. The other players must decide if they want to challenge. If no one challenges, the game continues. If someone wants to challenge, he or she calls out, "I doubt it." The card is then turned over to see what its actual value is. If it is the right card, the challenger must add all of the cards in the center to his or her hand. But, if it is not the card, the player who claimed that it was must pick up all of the cards in the center and add them to his or her hand. The first person to discard all of his or her cards is the winner.

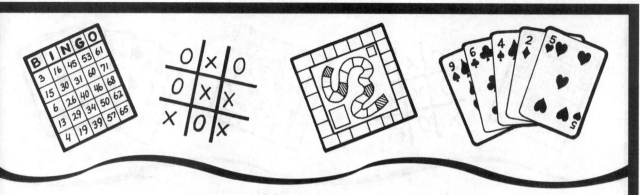

Pass the Present

Equipment:
- a small prize
- gift wrap
- scissors
- tape
- radio, record player, or cassette player

Where to Play:

indoors

Number of Players:

four or more

Directions:

Before the game begins, wrap the gift in 10 or more layers of gift wrap and select a leader. Have the players sit in a circle. When the leader starts the music, the players pass the present around the circle as quickly as possible. When the music stops (the leader should stop the music randomly, without looking) the player holding the present is allowed to remove one layer of paper. The music is started again and stopped until the gift has been completely unwrapped. The player who takes off the last layer of paper gets to keep the prize.

Word Lightning

Equipment:
- a watch or clock with a second hand

Where to Play:

anywhere

Number of Players:

two or more

Directions:

One player assigns another player a letter. The second player has one minute to call out as many words as possible that begin with that letter. The first player keeps count and watches the time. When there are more than two players, one player can keep count of the words, and the other player can watch the clock. After each player has had a turn, the player with the most words is the winner.

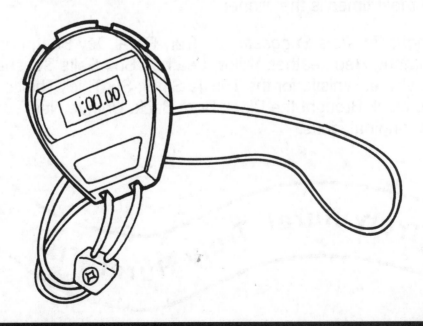

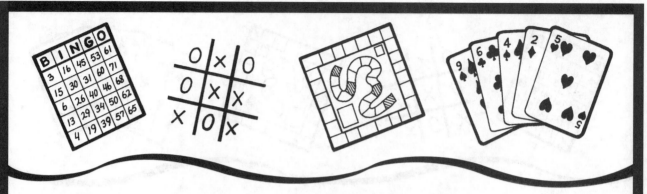

Tongue Twisters

Equipment:

• a watch or clock with a second hand

Where to Play:

anywhere

Number of Players:

two or more

Directions:

The object of this game is to repeat a tongue twister as many times as possible without making a mistake. One player chooses a tongue twister for the other player to say. The player is given one minute to recite the twister as many times as he or she can. Meanwhile, the partner who assigned the twister keeps track of how many times it is said and watches the time. The player who is able to clearly say it the most times is the winner.

Tongue Twisters Suggestions: Truly Rural, Toy Boat, Lemon Liniment, Red Leather, Yellow Leather, She Sells Seashells by the Seashore, Whistle for the Thistle Sifter, Six Thick Thistle Sticks, The Bootblack Brought the Black Boot Back, Unique New York, or your own original ideas.

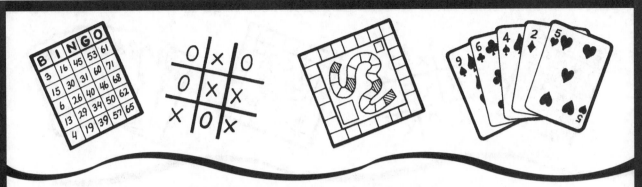

Western Union

Equipment:
- none

Where to Play:

anywhere

Number of Players:

eight or more

Directions:

Choose a person to be "it." He or she stands in the center of the circle that the other players form. "It" covers his or her eyes. One player announces that he or she is going to send a telegram to someone else in the circle. "I am going to send a telegram to (the name of another player in the circle)." Once this is announced, the player squeezes the hand of a player on either side. "It" opens his or her eyes and tries to catch a player squeezing another player's hand. The direction can be changed at any time. If a player is caught, he or she becomes "it." If the player who was announced as the recipient of the telegram gets the message (in the form of a squeeze), he or she announces so, and the process must begin again until "it" catches someone.

Milk Jug Drop

Equipment:
- empty, plastic, gallon milk jugs
- wooden clothespins

Where to Play:

anywhere

Number of Players:

two or more

Directions:

Before beginning this game, determine the distance that a player's hand can be from the jug when dropping clothespins. Divide the players into teams. Pass out an equal number of clothespins to each player. The players stand directly over the milk jugs and try to drop the clothespins into them. After all have dropped their clothespins, count the number in each jug. The team with the highest number of pins in their jug wins.

134

© Teacher Created Materials, Inc.

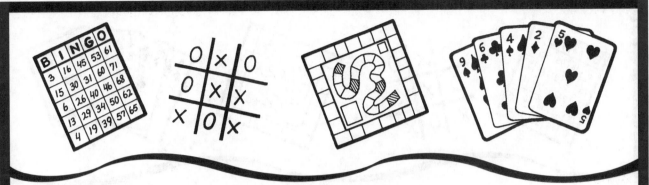

Battleship

Equipment:
- two pieces of paper for each player (Graph paper can be used, but it's not necessary.)
- pencils

Where to Play:

at a table

Number of Players:

two or four, if playing in partners

Directions:

The object of this game is to sink your opponent's battleships by making the right hits on a grid. Before beginning, the players need to draw their naval battlefield grids. Each player should draw two grids of 10 blocks down and 10 blocks across for a total of 100 blocks. The blocks do not need to be very big—a quarter of an inch (.64 cm) is large enough. The blocks should be numbered 1 through 10 along the top row of the grid. The left edge of the grid should be labeled with the letters A through J. One grid should be labeled for the player and the other for the opponent. Players then must place battleships on their own grids by drawing lines through consecutive blocks to indicate their ships' positions. Each player has four ships: an aircraft carrier of four blocks, a cruiser of three blocks, and two destroyers of two blocks apiece. The players mark their battleships on the grids without letting each other see the positions. The blocks must be located in straight lines horizontally, vertically, or diagonally. A battleship may not be split up.

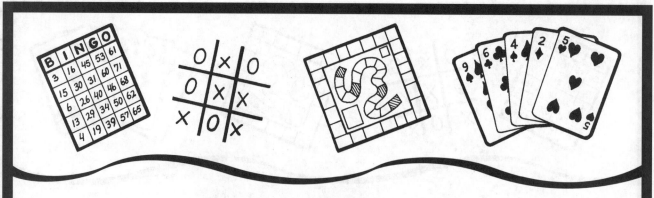

Battleship *(cont.)*

Directions *(cont.)*:

When the grids are drawn and the battleships are in place, the players should determine who fires first. Whoever begins gets 11 shots to hit the other player's battleships. The player calls out blocks on the grid according to their letters and numbers (for example C-9 or G-8) until he or she has used 11 shots. As the shots are being fired, the defensive player should mark them on his or her own grid with the number 1. This represents the first round. The firing player should also keep track of where his or her shots are fired by marking 1 on his or her second grid for the enemy. After all 11 shots have been fired, the defensive player calls out each shot and says whether it was a hit or a miss. It is considered a hit if it is on one of the squares marked for a battleship, and it is a miss if it is on an empty square. Players should circle the squares that are hit to distinguish them from misses. The process is repeated for the second player.

During the second round each player gets 11 shots minus the hits he or she scored in the first round. If a player made four hits, then he or she is allowed only seven shots in the second round. The number 2 is used to mark the shots made in the second round. Once all of the blocks constituting a ship have been hit, the player announces that the battleship is sunk. The game is over once all of a player's battleships have been sunk.

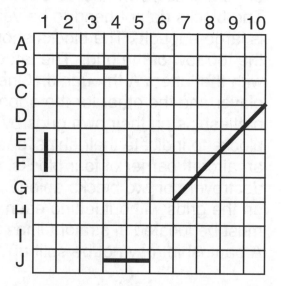

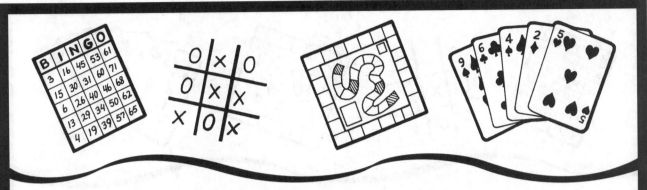

Clockwise Dice

Equipment:
- two dice
- paper
- a pencil

Where to Play:

at a table

Number of Players:

two or more

Directions:

The object of this game is to be the first player to roll the numbers 1 through 12 in the correct order. Roll one die to determine who goes first; the highest number starts. The first player rolls both dice in an attempt to roll a 1. If he or she is successful, the first number in that player's sequence has been completed. He or she may continue rolling to get the subsequent numbers until the dice fail to show a correct number. If the player does not roll a 1, then he or she must pass along the dice to the next player and wait for another turn. For the numbers through 6, both dice may be added together in order to earn the appropriate number. It is also possible for a player to score two numbers in one throw. For example, if a player rolls a 4 and a 5, then the next number needed in the sequence would be a 6. The numbers 7 through 12 must be obtained by adding the numbers on the dice together. The first player to roll 1 through 12 wins.

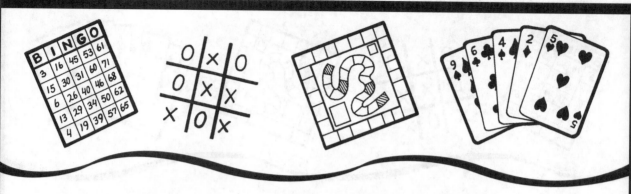

Square Tic-Tac-Toe

Equipment:

- a pencil
- paper
- 10 coins (You will need five of two different types, for example, five pennies and five nickels.)

Where to Play:

at a table

Number of Players:

two at a time

Directions:

Give each player a set of five coins that are the same. Choose one player to go first. Draw a square grid of nine equal boxes. The two players take turns placing one coin at a time on the grid. The first player to place three coins in a row—across, up or down, or diagonally—wins the game.

Concentration

Equipment:
- a deck of playing cards

Where to Play:

at a table

Number of Players:

two or more

Directions:

Shuffle the cards and lay them facedown in an orderly fashion. The first player turns over two cards so that everyone can see them, hoping to find a matching pair. If the cards match (two queens, for example), the player picks up the cards and gets another turn. If the cards do not match, then they must be placed facedown in their same positions, and the next person is given a turn. The players must concentrate to remember the locations of the cards. The game gets more exciting as more cards have been turned over and looked at. Once all of the matches have been made, the player with the most matches wins the game. The game can be made easier by using only part of the deck, thereby limiting the number of matches available.

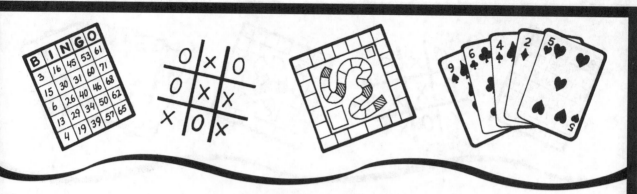

Fifty Points

Equipment:
- two dice
- a pencil
- paper

Where to Play:

at a table

Number of Players:

two or more

Directions:

Each player rolls one die to determine the order of play; the highest roller goes first. The first player rolls both dice. A score is made only when doubles are thrown. Two ones equal two points, two twos equal four points, two fours equal eight points, and two fives equal 10 points. To make the game interesting, two sixes equal 25 points, and two threes wipes out a player's total point tally. After the first player has rolled once, the next player is given a turn. The game is over when one player reaches or goes over 50 points.

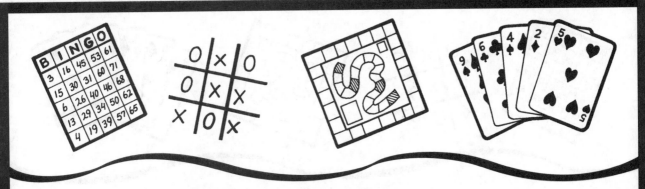

Going to Boston

Equipment:
- three dice
- paper
- a pencil

Where to Play:

at a table

Number of Players:

three or more

Directions:

The object of this game is to score the highest number of points by rolling the dice. Each player has three rolls per turn. All three dice are rolled at once, and the player sets aside the die with the highest value. The remaining two dice are rolled, and the player again sets aside the die with the highest value. The final die is then rolled. The sum of the three dice equals the player's score for that round. When all of the players have had a chance to roll a turn in the round, the play is over. The winner is the person with the highest score for that round. The number of rounds should be determined ahead of time. The overall winner is the person with the most points at the end of all of the rounds.

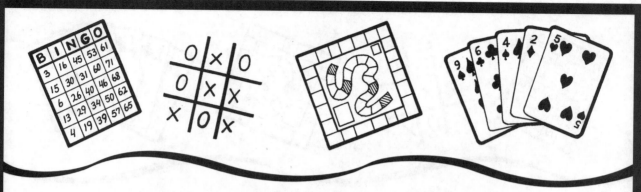

Guess the Number

Equipment:
- none

Where to Play:

anywhere

Number of Players:

two

Directions:

The object of this game is to guess the number your opponent has chosen. Specify a range of numbers, according to the ages and abilities of the players (for example, 1 to 10 or 1 to 100). The first player chooses a number within the designated range of numbers. Once the number has been chosen, the second player begins guessing the number. The second player makes a guess, and the first player indicates whether the guess is higher or lower than the actual number. The first player should keep track of the number of guesses made. When the second player guesses the correct number, the roles change. The player who guesses the number in the fewest tries is the winner.

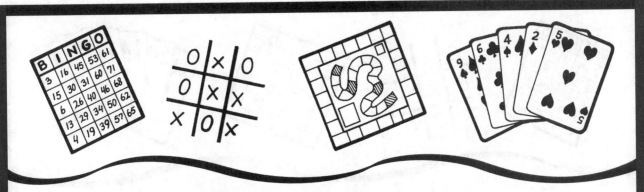

Math Baseball

Equipment:
- none

Where to Play:

anywhere

Number of Players:

10

Directions:

Create a small playing field by placing four bases about six to eight feet (1.8 to 2.4 m) apart in the shape of a baseball diamond. Divide the players into two equal teams. One team takes the field as the pitcher, catcher, and first, second, and third base player. The other team is the batting team. The first batter steps up to home plate, and the pitcher calls out a multiplication problem. (The problem should be appropriate for the skill and age level of the players.) One example is 5 x 3. The catcher and batter answer at the same time. If the batter answers first, then he or she advances to first base. If the catcher answers first, then the batter is out. The next player who comes to bat is given a problem and either advances or is called out. If the batter answers correctly, then any other players on the bases get to advance. The pitcher can try to put runners out by calling out problems to them. If the baseman answers correctly, then the runner is out. If the runner answers correctly, then he gets to advance by stealing a base. The teams switch places after three outs. The players can change positions from inning to inning so that others get a chance to be the pitcher. The team with the most runs at the end of nine innings wins the game. This game can be played with fewer innings.

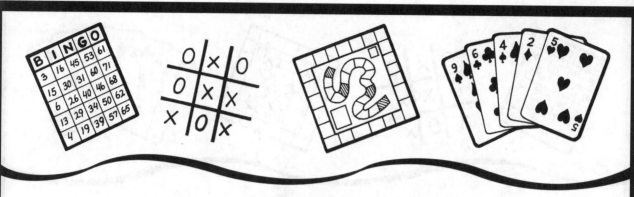

Buzz

Equipment:

• none

Where to Play:

anywhere

Number of Players:

two or more

Directions:

The object of this game is to count to 100 while substituting the word "buzz" for the number seven or any multiple of seven. Players line up and take turns counting, each player saying one number at a time. For example, the players would count to 20 as follows: 1, 2, 3, 4, 5, 6, buzz, 8, 9, 10, 11, 12, 13, buzz, 15, 16, buzz (because 17 has a seven in it), 18, 19, 20. When a player misses, the group must start counting at one again.

1 2 3 4 5 6 Buzz

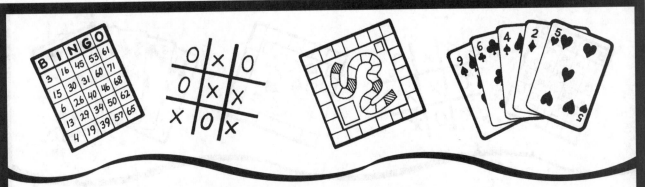

Spelling Bee

Equipment:
- a list of words appropriate for the age and skill levels of the players
- a dictionary

Where to Play:

anywhere

Number of Players:

two or more

Directions:

An adult should serve as the spelling master. The game starts when the spelling master gives the first player a word to spell. If the player spells it correctly, he or she gets a point. If the word is spelled incorrectly, the next player takes a turn. He or she is given a different word to spell. At the beginning of the game, the number of rounds should be determined. The player with the most points at the end of the last round is the winner. Spelling Bee can also be played as an elimination game. If a player does not spell a word correctly, he or she must leave the game. The last remaining player is the winner of the game. If there are enough players, this game can also be played in teams.

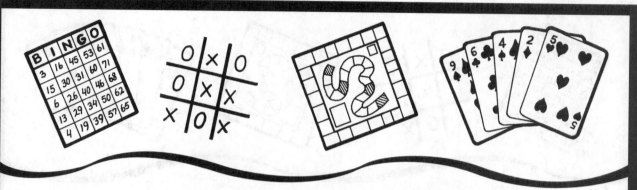

Action Spelling

Equipment:
- none

Where to Play:

anywhere

Number of Players:

two or more

Directions:

In this variation of the traditional spelling bee, actions will replace certain letters. Before starting the game, have the players choose which letters will be replaced by actions and what the actions will be. This will vary according to the ages and abilities of the participants. Younger players may start with just three replacements, and it is helpful if the actions begin with corresponding letters (such as a clap for the letter *c* or a jump for the letter *j).* Older players should be able to start with five to seven letters. For example, if the word is "jack" the student should jump, say the letter *a,* clap, and say the letter *k.* If a player misspells a word, he or she is eliminated. This game could be played for points instead of elimination by awarding a point each time a player correctly spells a word.

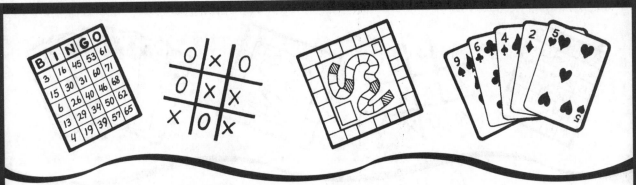

Aesop's Mission

Equipment:
- none

Where to Play:

anywhere

Number of Players:

four or more

Directions:

The object of this game is to discover the letter that Aesop has forbidden before being eliminated from the game. Assign roles to the players. One player is Aesop, and the other players are animals from Aesop's fables. Aesop secretly chooses a letter that must be avoided by the others. Aesop then asks a player a question that can only be answered with one word, hoping that the answer given will contain the secret letter. For example, if the secret letter is *p*, Aesop may ask the player what his or her favorite color is in the hope that the player will say "pink" or "purple." If the player responds with a word containing the secret letter, he or she loses a life. The next player gets a chance to guess what the secret letter is before being asked a question. A player is dropped or eliminated from the game after losing three lives. The players try to guess the secret letter before losing all three of their lives. The player who guesses the secret letter becomes the next Aesop.

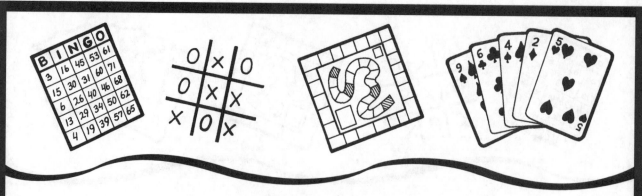

Charades

Equipment:
- paper
- a pencil
- a clock or watch with a second hand

Where to Play:

anywhere

Number of Players:

six or more

Directions:

The object of Charades is to guess, in the shortest time possible, the famous phrase or sentence being acted out by your team. After two teams are formed, one acts as the audience and the other as the actors. Each member of the audience writes a famous saying or title on a slip of paper. The phrase should be one that everyone will recognize. The phrases are put in a bowl and mixed up. An actor draws one paper at a time from the bowl and tries to act out the phrase through gestures to his or her teammates. These are some of the gestures used during charades:

- Hands held together with palms open means the clue is a book title.
- Arm bent at the elbow with the fist closed, moving in a circular motion means the clue is a movie title.
- The number of fingers held up indicates how many words are in the clue. Then the actor can hold up fingers indicating which word he or she is trying to act out.

© *Teacher Created Materials, Inc.*

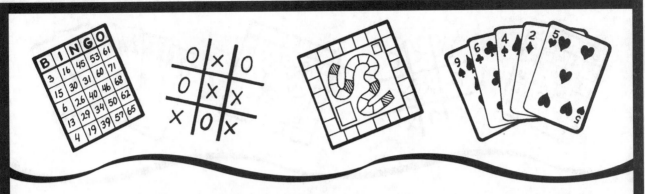

Charades *(cont.)*

- A hand cupped over the ear indicates the word "sounds like . . . ."
- A beckoning motion means the team is getting close to the right answer. If the team is far off, the actor makes a pushing gesture.

The team yells out guesses the whole time the actor is gesturing. A timekeeper keeps track of how long it takes the team to guess the right answer. If the team does not guess in the allotted amount of time, then they are given the total time in points. For example, if the teams decide that they will have one minute to guess and are not able to guess the right answer during that time, they are given 60 points. If they are able to guess in 45 seconds, then they are given 45 points. The team who has the least total guessing time (and points) wins the game.

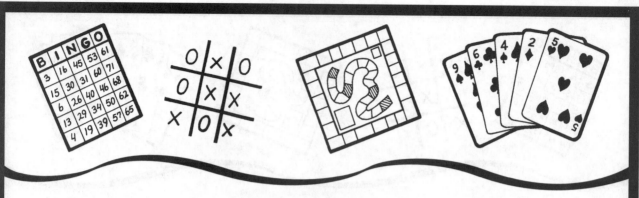

Coffeepot

Equipment:
- none

Where to Play:

anywhere

Number of Players:

three or more

Directions:

The object of the game is for "it" to guess the verb known to all of the other players. Choose one player to be "it." Ask another player to choose a verb and whisper it to all of the other players. When everyone but "it" knows the selected verb, "it" starts asking questions to try to discover the verb. He or she substitutes the word "coffeepot" for the unknown verb in the questions. For example, the word is swim, and "it" asks "Do you 'coffeepot' outside?" The players would respond "Yes." This continues until the verb is guessed or until a two- or three-minute time limit has been exceeded.

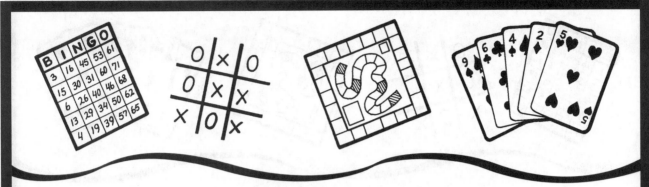

Stairway

Equipment:
- a pencil for each player
- paper

Where to Play:

anywhere

Number of Players:

two or more

Directions:

In this game, the players try to form stairways of words of increasing length from a given letter. To begin the game, one player selects a letter. Each player, on his or her own piece of paper, should try to form words by adding one letter at a time to the original letter. A time limit should be set. Five or ten minutes would be adequate.

If the letter is *m*, a player's stairway might look like the sample on the right:

```
m
me
men
mass
miles
musket
masters
monsters
monstrous
missionary
```

The builder of the longest stairway wins the game.

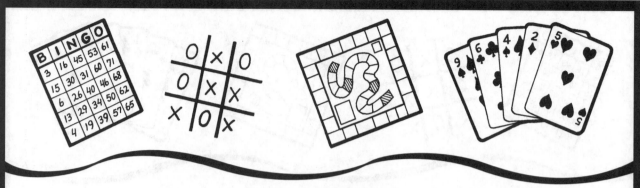

Crambo

Equipment:
- none

Where to Play:

anywhere

Number of Players:

six or more

Directions:

The object of this game is to guess the word chosen by one of the players. One player secretly chooses a word. If the word is "chair," the player will say, "I am thinking of a word that rhymes with bear." The rest of the players take turns asking questions in which they define words that rhyme with the given word. For example, if asked "Is it on your head?" the player would answer "No, it is not hair." "Is it like a carnival?" "No, it is not a fair." The first player to guess the correct word gets to choose the word for the next round.

I am thinking of a word
that rhymes with bear.

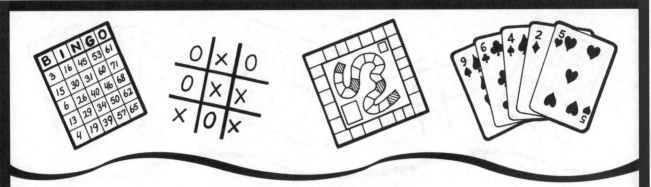

Crosswords

Equipment:
- a pencil for each player
- paper

Where to Play:

anywhere

Number of Players:

two or more

Directions:

On a sheet of paper, each player draws a square divided into 25 boxes (see below). The first player calls out any letter. Each player then places the letter in any box of his or her square. The players take turns calling out other letters that must also be placed on the squares. As the players place the letters, they should keep in mind that they are trying to form words. Once enough letters have been chosen to fill the diagrams, scoring is done as follows:

- Horizontal and vertical words score one point for each letter.

- A five-letter word scores a bonus point.

- Two separate words can be formed in one line and are worth one point for each letter, but words that can be split into separate words (like cabin which can be separated into cab and in) may only be scored once.

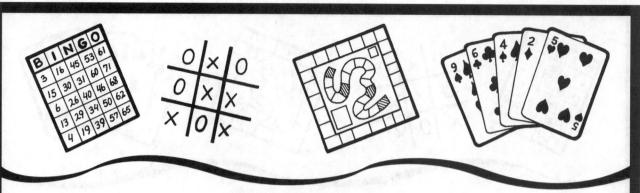

Hangman

Equipment:
- paper
- a pencil

Where to Play:

anywhere

Number of Players:

two or more

Directions:

Choose a player to be the hangman. He or she selects a word and draws a line for each letter, of the word on a piece of paper. For example, if the word has five letters then five blank lines are drawn. The first player tries to guess a letter that may be in the word. If it is one of the letters, the hangman puts the letter on the appropriate line or lines. If a player makes an incorrect guess, the hangman starts to draw the gallows and the man.

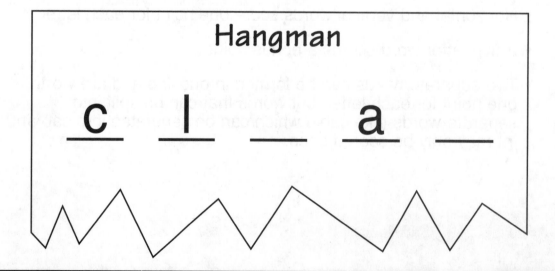

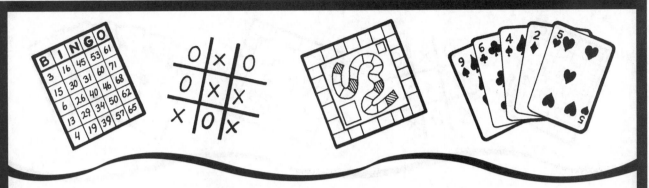

Hangman *(cont.)*

The drawing is created as follows:

Incorrect Guesses	Drawing Addition
1	the line at the base of the gallows
2	the upright line
3	the arm beam
4	the support beam
5	the rope
6	the figure's head
7	the body
8	the right arm
9	the left arm
10	the right leg
11	the left leg

The hangman wins if the left leg has been drawn and the word has not been correctly guessed.

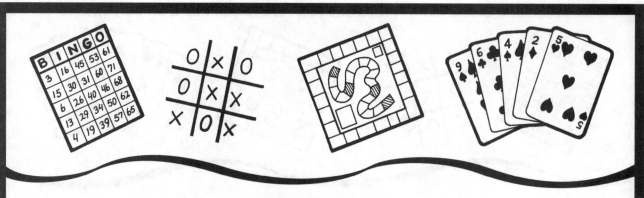

Initials

Equipment:
- none

Where to Play:

anywhere

Number of Players:

two or more

Directions:

Select a player to be the questioner for the first round. The questioner takes turns asking each player a question. The players answer the questions by using words formed with their own initials. If the questioner asks, "What is your favorite food, Harrison Postler?" Harrison may reply "hot pizza." The answers do not need to make sense. The silly replies make the game more fun.

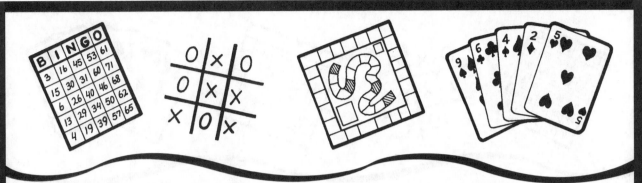

Letters by Number

Equipment:
- none

Where to Play:

anywhere

Number of Players:

three or more

Directions:

Choose a player to be the caller. He or she starts the game by calling out a number between 1 and 26. The other players try to be the first to find the corresponding letter of the alphabet (1 = A, 2 = B, 11 = K, and so on). The alphabet and its corresponding numbers should be written out for the caller. A wrong answer results in the loss of a point. A right answer earns a point. The game can be played for a certain length of time or until a certain number of points has been reached.

A	B	C	D	E	F	G	H	I	J	K	L	M	N	O	P	Q	R	S	T	U	V	W	X	Y	Z
1	2	3	4	5	6	7	8	9	10	11	12	13	14	15	16	17	18	19	20	21	22	23	24	25	26

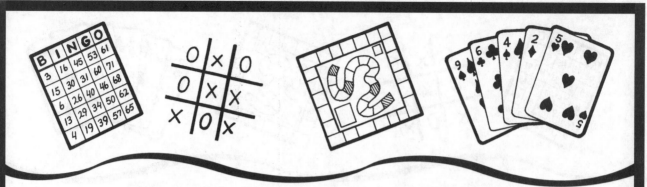

Magazine Storytelling

Equipment:
- old magazines
- scissors
- glue
- paper
- crayons
- pencils
- stapler and staples

Where to Play:

anywhere

Number of Players:

two or more

Directions:

This game may be played individually or in teams. Give each player or team a set of the following materials: old magazines, scissors, paper, glue, crayons, and a pencil. Within a certain period of time, 10 or 15 minutes, the players must put together stories from pictures and words cut out of magazines. These clippings should be glued on paper to form the pages of a book. After the time period has elapsed, staple the books together, and have the players read their books out loud. The stories can be judged based on the following categories: most clever, best use of the pictures, funniest, etc. To make the game easier, a topic could be chosen before beginning.

Rigmarole

Equipment:
- none

Where to Play:

anywhere

Number of Players:

three or more

Directions:

Rigmarole is a game that tests the memory and offers tongue twisting enjoyment. The first player starts the game by creating an alliterative phrase of three words that begin with *o* for the number "one." An example would be "Our own ostrich . . . ." The next player starts by saying the first person's phrase, and then he or she creates another phrase beginning with *t* for the number two. The string of phrases continues around the circle until 10 have been created.

The Minister's Cat

Equipment:
- none

Where to Play:

anywhere

Number of Players:

two or more

Directions:

The object of this game is to describe and name the minister's cat with one adjective and name for every letter in the alphabet. The first player begins the game by forming a sentence, using the following formula: "The minister's cat is a(n)_____ cat, and his name is_____." The first blank is replaced with an adjective that begins with the letter *a*, and the second blank is replaced with a name that begins with the letter *a*. The first sentence might be, "The minister's cat is an *active* cat, and his name is *Andy.*" The next player must do the same, also using the letter *a*. Once the round has been completed, the players use the letter *b*. After each round the group proceeds to the next letter of the alphabet. A player must drop out if he or she repeats a word or is unable to think of a word.

Note: You can determine the length of a round. It can be considered complete when everyone has had a chance or when a player cannot come up with any more options for the letter. Use parameters that work best for you.

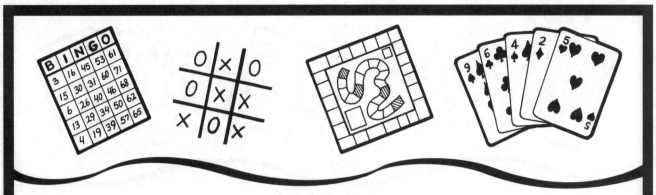

Sneeze

Equipment:
- none

Where to Play:

anywhere

Number of Players:

six or more

Directions:

If this activity is done correctly, the end result should be a loud sound that resembles a sneeze. The leader whispers a syllable (ash, ish, osh, or choo) in each player's ear. It is important that each player remembers his or her syllable. At the count of three, have everyone call out their sounds in unison as loudly as they can. It should sound like a very loud sneeze.

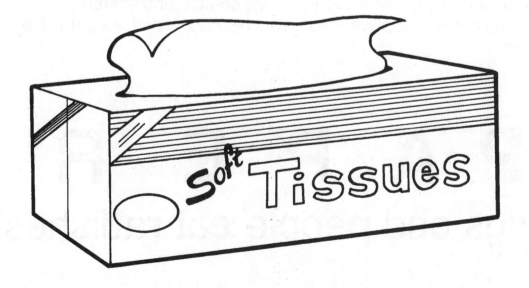

Sentences

Equipment:
- paper
- pencils

Where to Play:

anywhere

Number of Players:

three or more

Directions:

One player chooses a word to be used in the first round. The word should be five or six letters long. Each player must create a sentence of words which begin with the letters in the original word. For example, if the word is "paper," a sentence could be "Pigs and people eat radishes." The letters must stay in the same order as in the original word. After everyone has created and shared a sentence, the next player chooses a new word, and the game begins again.

P A P E R

Pigs **a**nd **p**eople **e**at **r**adishes.

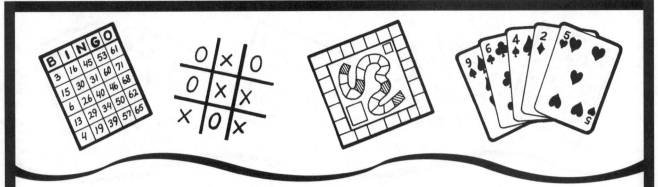

Botticelli

Equipment:
 • none

Where to Play:
anywhere

Number of Players:
three or more

Directions:
One player chooses a famous person who would be familiar to all of the players. He or she then reveals the initial of the secret person's last name. The other players try to guess who the secret person is by asking questions phrased in such a way that the chooser must identify other people with the same initial. For example, if the initial is *J*, a question might be "Are you one of the fathers of the Constitution?" The chooser must answer with the name of one of the fathers of the Constitution whose name begins with *J* or answer a forfeit question. If the chooser can answer "No, I am not Thomas Jefferson," then the next player asks a question. If a player is able to stump the chooser, then he or she can ask more specific questions: "Are you female?" ("No, I am not female.") or "Are you dead?" ("No, I am not dead.") Only yes or no answers are allowed. The players continue to ask questions until the identity has been revealed. The player who guesses the identity of the secret person gets to choose the secret person for the next round.

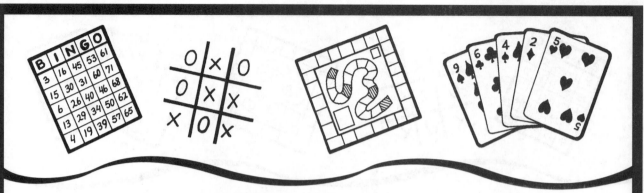

Categories

Equipment:
- paper
- pencils

Where to Play:

anywhere

Number of Players:

four or more

Directions:

Before beginning, set a time limit for the game, and create a list of about 20 science or social studies categories. Each person can contribute four or five category ideas. Have the players each list all of the categories at the top of a sheet of paper. A player chooses any letter at random. (A different letter is picked for each round.) During the allotted time (five or ten minutes), each player writes as many words as possible that begin with the chosen letter and belong in each category. When the time limit is up, the players exchange their lists for scoring. The answers are read aloud. Each answer is worth one point. If a player uses an answer that no one else thought of, he or she gets two points.

Mystery Word

Equipment:
- paper
- pencil

Where to Play:

anywhere

Number of Players:

five

Directions:

The object of this game is to help your partner guess the mystery word by giving him or her synonyms or related word clues. Choose one person to be the quiz master. The other four players split into two pairs. The quiz master chooses a word that he or she discreetly passes on to just one player from each pair. The word can either be whispered or written down on small slips of paper. The player chosen to go first gives his or her partner a one word clue that is a synonym or a word related to the secret word. If the player cannot think of a clue, he or she may pass. For example, if the word is "basketball," the first clue might be "game." If the partner guesses correctly, the team gets one point. If not, the next team has a turn. When the word is guessed, the partners switch roles. A time limit should be set. At the end of the specific period of time, the team with the most points wins. At this time, the quiz master can trade places with one of the players.

Taste

Equipment:
- paper cups
- a variety of drinks
- a blindfold
- paper
- pencil

Where to Play:
anywhere

Number of Players:
three or more

Directions:
Blindfold a player, and give him or her a variety of beverages to identify by taste. The greater the variety, the more challenging the game. Soda, juice, sparkling water, etc., can be used. A second player records the taster's answers. The player who identifies the most drinks is the winner. If the taster is able to identify brand names, award extra points. This is a great game to play after an active outdoor game.

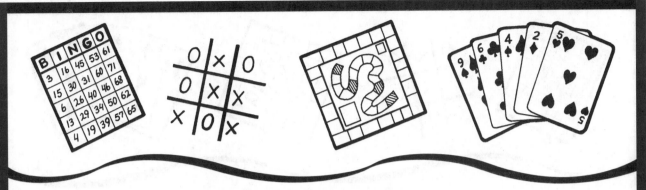

Musical Chairs

Equipment:
- a chair for every player except one
- music

Where to Play:

a large enough area to accommodate all of the chairs

Number of Players:

six or more

Directions:

Place the chairs in a straight line, alternating the directions they are facing. Choose a leader, and spread out the players evenly around the chairs. When the leader has started the music, the players should walk in one direction around the chairs. The leader stops the music after a short amount of time has elapsed. The moment the music stops, the players scramble to find places to sit. The one player left without a chair is eliminated from the game. Remove one of the chairs to keep the number of chairs fewer than the players. Repeat the process. The game is over when only one player is left with a chair.

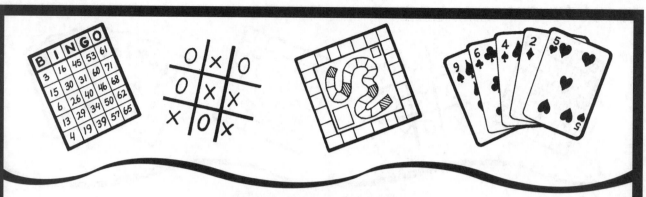

Orchestra

Equipment:
- none

Where to Play:

anywhere

Number of Players:

five or more

Directions:

In this game the players' goal is to follow the motions of the orchestra leader. Choose a player to be the conductor. The players, including the conductor, each choose a musical instrument that they will pretend to play. The players and the conductor sit in a circle with about one foot between each person. The conductor starts the game by pretending to play his or her instrument. Then the other players start making the movements associated with the instruments they have chosen. Once everyone is playing his or her imaginary instruments, the conductor switches to the actions of one of the other instruments being played by another orchestra member. The other players must be paying attention because they too need to start playing that instrument. The player whose instrument is now being imitated must stop and cover his or her ears. After a short time, the conductor returns to his or her original instrument, and the rest of the players do the same. Then the conductor changes to another instrument, and the process begins again. A player is eliminated from a game when he or she makes an incorrect motion. The last remaining player in the game is the winner and becomes the conductor.

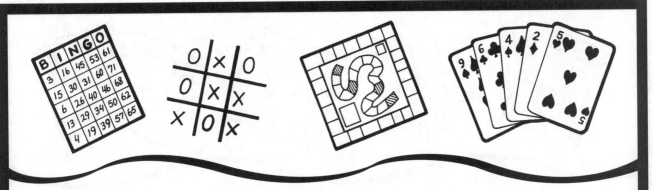

Rain

Equipment:
- none

Where to Play:

anywhere

Number of Players:

three or more

Directions:

Have the players sit quietly in a circle with their eyes closed. The leader starts the rainstorm by rubbing the palms of his or her hands together. The player to the left of the leader joins in. Then the player to the left of the second player joins in, and so on. When everyone has joined in, the leader changes the sound by snapping his or her fingers. The process begins again. Once all are snapping their fingers, the leader changes to slapping his or her thighs. This is the sound of heavy rain. Thunder can be added by players stomping their feet on the floor. The sound reaches its peak at this point. The leader then does the sounds in the reverse order. The leader may have to gently nudge the player on his or her left because it can be very loud at this point, and the players should still have their eyes closed. The group follows the leader back through the motions until the room is again in complete silence.

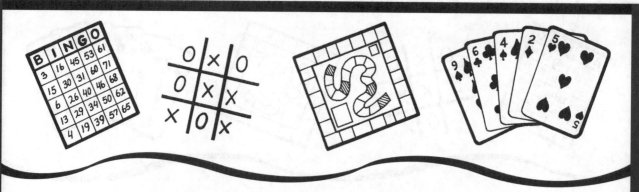

Art Consequences

Equipment:
- paper
- pencils

Where to Play:

at a table

Number of Players:

three

Directions:

In this game, a group of three players will cooperate to draw an imaginary figure. Start by dividing the players into groups of three. The first player secretly draws a head and neck on the upper third of a sheet of paper. The paper is then folded so that the next player cannot see the head but can see part of the neck. The next player draws the shoulders, the arms, and torso. When the second player is finished, he or she folds the paper so that only the bottom edge of the drawing is showing. The drawing is finished by the third player. After the legs are drawn, the paper is unfolded to reveal the entire picture. If there is more than one group there can be a competition for the silliest, scariest, most realistic, etc.

170

© Teacher Created Materials, Inc.

Musical Clapping

Equipment:
- none

Where to Play:

anywhere

Number of Players:

two or more

Directions:

The object of this game is to guess the song by its clapped rhythm. Choose one player to be the clapper. He or she thinks of a common song that all of the players will know. The clapper claps the rhythm to the secret song. The players call out their answers when they think they recognize the song. The player who guesses correctly gets to be the next clapper.

Holiday Games

Explorers Come Along

Equipment:
- one less chair than the number of players
- music

Where to Play:

indoors

Number of Players:

five or more

Directions:

Choose one player to be the leader. Have the players sit in chairs in a circle. While music is played, the leader (Christopher Columbus), walks around the inside of the circle, extending a hand. The seated players choose whether to take the hand or not. When a seated player takes the hand and joins the leader, that player joins Christopher Columbus on a voyage of exploration. That player, or new explorer, extends his or her other hand to the seated players. More and more players join the group of explorers as they walk, holding hands, around the inside of the circle. When the music stops, all of the explorers let go of each other's hands and rush for a seat. The explorer left without a seat becomes the new Christopher Columbus and starts a new voyage of discovery.

Treasure Hunt

Equipment:
- two brown paper bags
- tape
- treats

Where to Play:

indoors or outdoors

Number of Players:

five or more

Directions:

The leader crumples the paper bags and then flattens them out. A treasure map is drawn on one of the bags. The other bag is torn into pieces to be used for the clues. After the leader decides where to hide the treasure (candy, pencils, or other inexpensive treats), the map is drawn. Clues are written and numbered. (Example: Find the tree that has a split. Stand on your toes and reach for it.) The leader hides the map and all of the clues except for clue number one. Clue number one will lead to where clue number two is. Clue number two will lead to where clue number three is, and so on. The last clue leads to the map. The leader gives clue number one to the players/explorers. The explorers must find the clues in order and find the map. The map will lead the explorers to the treasure.

Quick-Draw Columbus

Equipment:
- slips of paper
- chalkboard and chalk
- timer

Where to Play:

indoors

Number of Players:

five or more

Directions:

Before the game begins, the leader writes words related to Christopher Columbus and other explorers on slips of paper. (Examples include *Niña, Pinta, Santa Maria, Spain, queen, America, ocean, map, ship*, or any other related words and terms which have been studied in class.) The slips of paper are placed in a hat, bowl, or other container. The players are divided into two teams. A player on the first team must randomly choose a slip of paper and draw on the chalkboard a picture that represents the word or phrase. No talking or gesturing is allowed. The player's teammates must try to guess the word or phrase before the time runs out (about one minute, depending upon the age of the group). Each team earns a point for a correct answer. Team members may also make up their own Columbus Day clues to challenge the other players.

Alone in the Wilderness

Equipment:
- none

Where to Play:

anywhere

Number of Players:

three or more

Directions:

Seat the players in a circle, and introduce the idea of surviving in the wilderness. Explain the following: You will be traveling alone, and you may bring only what you can carry on a walk. The first player names one item that he or she would need to survive on a wilderness journey. The second player in the circle must repeat the item that the first player said and add one of his or her own. The third players must repeat the items named by both the first and second player and add one of his or her own, and so on. The object of the game is to travel as far around the circle as possible without the players forgetting any of the survival items.

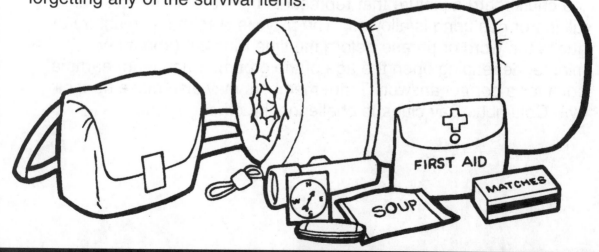

Columbus Day List Mania

Equipment:
- chalkboard and chalk
- paper
- pencils

Where to Play:

indoors by a chalkboard

Number of Players:

any number

Directions:

Choose a category before the game begins, and write it on the chalkboard. Then ask the players to write as many items as possible from the category. After a one- or two-minute time period, the winner is the player with the greatest number of appropriate answers. Here are some examples.

- List the names of the oceans.

- List the names of Columbus' ships.

- List words having to do with ships.

- List items that Columbus would have carried on his ships.

- List the things Columbus might have seen on his voyage.

- List some challenges faced by Columbus.

- Lists the names of as many explorers as you can.

Mummy Wrap

Equipment:
- toilet paper or crepe paper
- tape (optional)

Where to Play:
indoors

Number of Players:
four or more

Directions:
Divide the players into pairs. One partner in each pair needs to be the mummy, and the other partner needs to be the mummy wrapper. On the count of three, all of the mummy wrappers must race to wrap up their mummies with the rolls of toilet paper. To win, a mummy wrapper has to be the first to wrap his or her mummy from head to toe (except for the face). In the hurry and excitement of wrapping, players will soon find that the toilet paper easily tears, causing all kinds of delays and giggles. To make the mummy wrapping easier, provide tape.

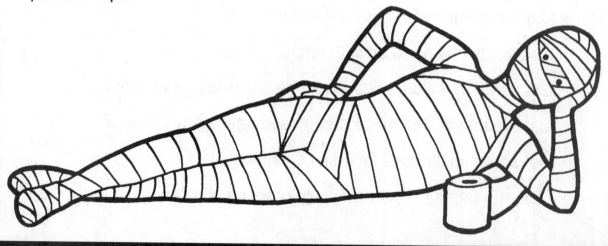

Investigation

Equipment:
- none

Where to Play:
indoors

Number of Players:
three or more

Directions:
The player whose last name starts with the letter nearest the end of the alphabet is the first to be the suspect. The suspect leaves the room and changes something about him or herself. For example, one might unbutton a button, loosen a belt, spray on some perfume, change a hairstyle, or untie a shoe. After the change has been made, the suspect goes back into the room where the other players are waiting. The first player to discover what has been changed becomes the next suspect.

Spider's Web

Equipment:
- a large piece of furniture or gym equipment
- black yarn

Where to Play:

indoors

Number of Players:

any number

Directions:

Place a large piece of furniture or gym equipment in the center of the room. String the yarn from the furniture to the other outlying furniture in the area to form a large spider web. Wrap the yarn around table legs, chairs, or shelves, and keep returning to the center. Be sure that the strings vary in height. Let the players (one to three at a time) take turns moving in and out of the spider's web while trying not to get stuck!

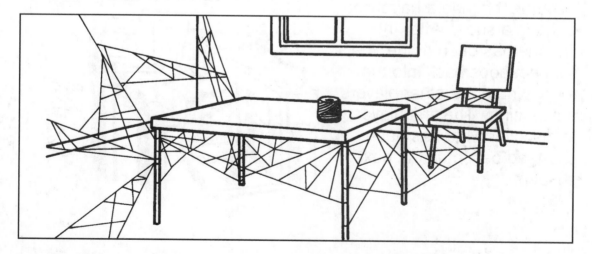

Box Bowling

Equipment:
- a ball
- six small boxes, covered with orange and black construction paper and numbered 1, 2, 3, 4, 5, and 6

Where to Play:
on a flat surface

Number of Players:
two or more

Directions:
Set up the boxes in a triangle shape with the point facing the players. The players roll the ball and knock over as many boxes as possible. The score is the total number on the knocked-over boxes. Decide before beginning how many turns each player will have.

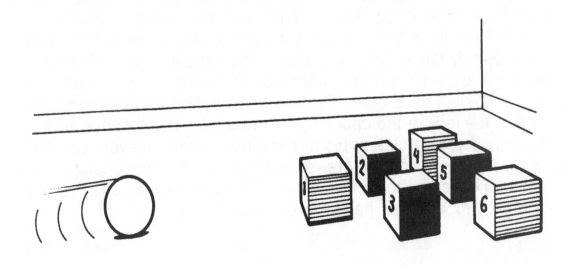

Broom Croquet

Equipment:
- two push brooms
- two chairs
- a rag

Where to Play:
outdoors or in a gym

Number of Players:
at least six

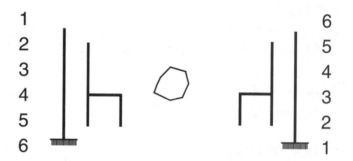

Directions:

Divide the players into two teams, and line them up against opposite walls (or lines, if you are outside), facing each other. Number off the players, starting at the right-hand end of each line. Therefore, the number ones will stand diagonally from each other at opposite ends of the room. Place one chair on the floor in front of each line. Put the push brooms on the floor next to the chairs with the handles parallel to the team lines. Place the rag midway between the chairs, at an equal distance from each side. Choose a leader. The leader calls out any player number. Both players with that number run and pick up their team's broom. The two players then try to push the rag between the legs of the opposing team's chair. The first player to succeed scores a point for his or her team. After a player scores a point, the brooms and rag are returned to their original positions, and the leader calls out another number. The game continues until most of the players, if not all, have had at least one turn.

Halloween Carols

Equipment:
- none

Where to Play:

anywhere

Number of Players:

any number

Directions:

In this activity the players (in teams) write Halloween songs. The songs can parody traditional Christmas carols or current popular songs, or they can be written from scratch. The following are some ideas:

- Shivery Yells (to the tune of "Jingle Bells")

- Spooky the Friendly Goblin (to the tune of "Rudolph the Red-Nosed Reindeer")

- Scary Hairy New Cremation Purple Polka Dot Mutation (to the tune of "Itsy Bitsy Teenie Weenie Yellow Polka Dot Bikini")

- Ghouls Creep In (to the tune of "Fools Rush In")

After every team has finished composing a song, have them perform their creations. The songs can be judged or just performed for each other's enjoyment.

When I Get to America

Equipment:
• none

Where to Play:
anywhere

Number of Players:
any number

Directions:
The first player begins by saying "When I get to America, I will . . ." and names something he or she will do. For example, ". . . I will build a house." The player to his or her left continues by saying "When I get to America, I will build a house and . . . ," adding his or her own phrase to the list. Each player, in turn, repeats what has already been said and adds one more thing. If a player forgets an item or does one out of order, he or she does not add to the list on that turn. However, the next time around the player has a chance to repeat what has gone before and to add his or her own part. As a variation to this game, the players can be required to act out what they will do in America.

When I get to America, I will build a house.

The Last of the Turkey

Equipment:
- pencils
- paper

Where to Play:

anywhere

Number of Players:

any number

Directions:

Call out the name of something related to Thanksgiving. If the word *cooking* is called out, the players must write it down and then try to think of another Thanksgiving word beginning with the last letter, for example, *gobble.* They then must think of a word beginning with the last letter of *gobble* (e), such as *eating.* After a designated amount of time, the winner is the player or team with the most listed words.

Turkey Vocabulary

Equipment:
- colored index cards
- pencils
- scissors

Where to Play:

anywhere

Number of Players:

four or more

Directions:

Divide the players into cooperative teams. Give each team a set of colored index cards. Have the teammates work together to write words related to Thanksgiving, Native Americans, explorers, or any other social studies or literature terms that they are familiar with. The players write a word on one half of a card and its definition on the other half. The card is then torn or cut in half. Each team should create a whole set of cards in this way. Collect the cards from all of the teams and then pass out a set to each team. (Make sure that the teams do not receive the sets that they created.) Allow two minutes for the teams to work on matching each word with its definition. The team with the most correct answers wins.

Who's Shaking the Beads?

Equipment:
- two blindfolds
- a small cardboard box containing a few dried peas or pebbles
- masking tape

Where to Play:

a large, open area

Number of Players:

eight or more

Directions:

Divide the players into pairs. Arrange the pairs in a circle and place one pair within the circle. Blindfold both of the people who are within the circle. Choose one of the blindfolded players to be the bead maker, and give him or her the box to hold. The other player is the bead trader. The bead maker holds the box and shakes it two or three times, in about 10-second intervals, as he or she moves around within the circle. The trader tries to find the bead maker by listening for the rattles. The bead maker tries to evade the trader by listening for his or her footsteps. Neither may move out of the circle of the other players. If one does, the game is stopped and begins again at the starting positions. If the trader is moving away from the bead maker, the players in the circle shout an agreed upon word such as "whoa!" The trader is given three minutes to touch the bead maker; then, another pair gets a turn inside of the circle.

Moccasin Guessing Game

Equipment:
- four shoes
- four smooth stones, one marked with paint or marker

Where to Play:

indoors, at a table

Number of Players:

four or more

Directions:

Divide the players into teams of two or three. Put the moccasins (shoes) in the center of the table, and have the players sit around the table. The first player takes the four stones, shakes them in his or her hands, and puts one stone in each moccasin. Meanwhile, the first player's teammates try to distract the other team from seeing which moccasin the marked stone is placed in by making funny faces, singing, telling jokes, etc. A person on the opposing team guesses which moccasin has the marked stone. If he or she is correct, the same team tries to again fool its opponents. If the guess is incorrect, the opposing team gets a chance to drop the stones in the moccasins in the same manner. The first team to correctly guess four times wins.

T . . . T . . . T . . . Turkey Tribute

Equipment:
- paper
- pencils

Where to Play:

indoors

Number of Players:

any number

Directions:

Give the players 10 minutes to make up as many sentences as possible that have at least five words beginning with the letter *T*. Have the players read their goofy sentences aloud. The person with the most sentences wins.

> The terrified turkeys danced the Turkey Trot on Thanksgiving day.

> Tim trained his tremendously talented tarantula to talk.

Hanukkah Categories

Equipment:
- none

Where to Play:

indoors

Number of Players:

three or more

Directions:

As a group, brainstorm a list of words that have to do with Hanukkah, such as menorah, Bible, Judaism, synagogue, and worship. Use an encyclopedia to search for as many words as possible. Have the players sit cross-legged in a circle. The first player begins a rhythm by slapping his or her legs twice, clapping twice, and snapping the fingers of his or her left hand and then right hand in an even rhythm. The rest of the players then join in the same rhythm until all of the players are in unison. The starting player then calls out a Hanukkah word, saying it just after he or she snaps, without changing or losing the rhythm. The next player in the circle follows, naming another word just after snapping. The game continues around the circle until a player cannot think of a word, repeats a word, or misses the beat. That player is out and must leave the circle. The game is over when only one player remains in the circle.

Chain Pantomime

Equipment:
- none

Where to Play:
anywhere

Number of Players:
five or more

Directions:
Choose five volunteers to be the actors and have the rest of the group sit in a semicircle. Ask the five volunteers to leave the room for a couple of minutes. While they are gone, the group determines a specific, Hanukkah-related action to be pantomimed in detail. This action might be, for example, wrapping a gift, lighting the candles of a menorah, or spinning a dreidle. One member of the audience agrees to clearly pantomime the idea. Then one of the five volunteers is called back to the group while the other four remain out of sight. The action is pantomimed for the volunteer who, in turn, attempts to repeat the pantomime for the next volunteer who is called back in. This volunteer repeats the pantomime for the next volunteer and so on until the fifth volunteer has returned and has had the opportunity to watch the action. The last volunteer then tries to guess what the original action was. By this time, the action may have undergone many changes. (Remind volunteers not to guess the pantomime orally. Only the last volunteer guesses the original action.) At the end, it is interesting to find out what each person was trying to do and then to demonstrate the original action for the benefit of those who were out of the room.

Menorah Game

Equipment:
- paper
- pencils
- markers
- poster board or cardstock

Where to Play:

indoors

Number of Players:

four

Directions:

Before the game begins, cut out 36 small, square cards from cardstock. On 32 of the cards draw menorahs. On four of these show a menorah with one candle, on another four show a menorah with two candles, and so on up to eight candles. On the remaining four blank cards draw the Star of David. Give each player a piece of paper on which to draw a large, nine-square grid. In the center of each grid the players should draw a Star of David, and the rest of the squares should be numbered 1 through 8. Place the 36 small cards facedown on the table. The players take turns picking a card and placing it on their boards. If a player picks a menorah card, he or she matches the number of candles in the menorah to the number in the square; if a player picks a Star of David card, he or she puts it in the middle square. If a player picks a card he or she already has, it should be put back at the bottom of the pile. The game continues until one or all of the players have filled their boards.

Light the Menorah

Equipment:
- poster board or cardstock
- paper
- yellow construction paper
- pencil
- scissors

Where to Play:

indoors

Number of Players:

any number

Directions:

Before the game begins, draw a large menorah on a piece of paper for each player, and cut out nine yellow flames for each menorah. Then make a set of game cards out of cardstock. On each card write one sentence about Hanukkah and underline one word of each sentence. Give every player a menorah card and nine flames. The first player draws a card and tries to identify the part of speech of the underlined word. If the answer is correct, the player places a flame on one of his or her candles. The first player to light all of his or her candles wins.

Santa's Sack

Equipment:

- a bag full of noisy, clanking things (such as empty soda cans or bells)
- blindfolds

Where to Play:

anywhere

Number of Players:

three or more

Directions:

One player plays the part of Santa while everyone else is blindfolded. Santa circulates among the blindfolded players. Everyone listens for Santa's sack and tries to grab it. The winner plays Santa in the next round.

What's inside Santa's Sack?

The Hidden Card

Equipment:
- assorted old Christmas cards

Where to Play:

indoors

Number of Players:

two or more

Directions:

Each player tears a card into six pieces and hides five of them around the room. He or she gives the last piece of the card to another player. The winner is the first player to find all of the pieces to his or her Christmas card jigsaw.

December Dictionary Dash

Equipment:
- dictionaries
- paper
- pencils

Where to Play:

indoors

Number of Players:

four or more

Directions:

Divide the players into teams of two or three. Challenge the players to find in the dictionary as many words as possible that relate to Christmas or Hanukkah. After 30 minutes, the team with the longest list wins, but they must be able to use all of their words in sentences.

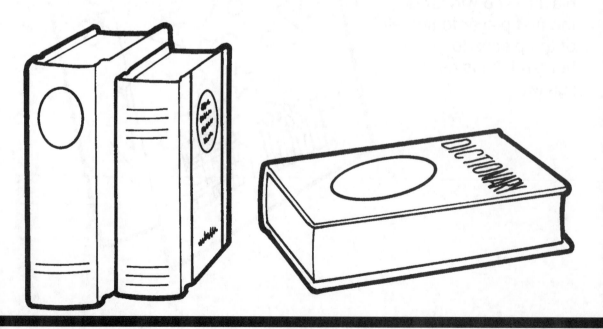

Santa Toss

Equipment:
- red balloons
- cotton balls
- permanent markers
- glue

Where to Play:

indoors

Number of Players:

any number

Directions:

Give each player a red balloon. Use a permanent marker to decorate a Santa face. Have the players glue cotton-ball beards onto their balloons. At the leader's signal, the players toss their Santa balloons into the air. The player who keeps his or her Santa in the air the longest wins.

Holiday Music Relay

Equipment:
- holiday music
- chairs (optional)

Where to Play:

indoors

Number of Players:

10 or more

Directions:

Divide the players into teams of five to eight players. Line them up, one behind the other. They may stand, squat on the floor, or sit in chairs. Mark a point about 20 feet (6 m) in front of each team. Assign a well-known holiday song to the first player in each team, such as "Jingle Bells," "Rudolph the Red-Nosed Reindeer," "Deck the Halls," etc. Assign a different song to player number two, number three, and so on. When one of these songs is played, the player in each team who has that song must rise, run forward and around the turning point, and return to his or her place. The first player back and in position after each song earns a point for his or her team. After all of the songs have been played, the team with the most points is the winner.

Santa, Santa Walk Around

Equipment:
- a Santa hat
- a small box wrapped as a gift

Where to Play:

an open area

Number of Players:

five or more

Directions:

Have the players sit in a circle. Designate one player to play the part of Santa. Santa carries a present and walks around the outside of the circle while the rest of the group chants "Santa, Santa, walk around. Santa put the present down." Santa gives the present to the player of his or her choice. The player must tag Santa before he can run around the circle and steal the player's seat. If Santa is able to sit down without being tagged, the player he chose becomes the new Santa, and the game begins again.

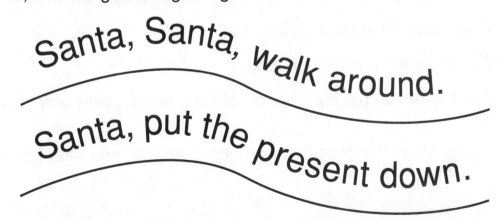

Santa, Santa, walk around.

Santa, put the present down.

Squishers

Equipment:
- large balloons
- fine sand or flour
- funnel
- spoon
- pencil

Where to Play:

indoors

Number of Players:

any number

Directions:

To make New Year's squisher balloons, pull the end of a balloon onto a funnel. Pour in a filling of sand or flour to fill the balloon. Poke it gently with a pencil to release from the funnel. Tap and squish the balloon to get rid of the air. Tie a knot, and pull it tight. Give one balloon to each player, and try some of the following games.

- Toss them! Play catch or baseball.

- Squish them! It just feels good.

- Kick them! Keep a squisher off of the ground, using only your feet.

- Juggle them! Practice first with one, then two, and then three squishers.

Balancing Beanbags

Equipment:
- one beanbag per player
- popular music from the passing year

Where to Play:

an open area

Number of Players:

three or more

Directions:

Give each player a beanbag. Play some of the most popular songs from the passing year and stop the music every once in a while. While the music is playing, the players dance and move. When the music stops, name a body part and have the players balance their beanbags on that part as they move. As the game continues, the speed of the music can be changed. For a variation, ask the players to take turns calling out body parts.

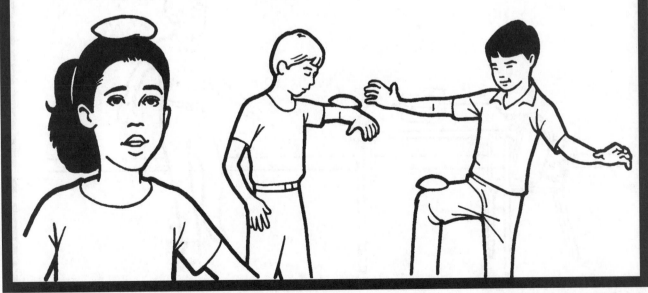

Ticktock

Equipment:
- an alarm clock

Where to Play:
indoors

Number of Players:
any number

Directions:
Before the game begins, set an alarm clock or kitchen timer to go off at a certain time. Hide the clock somewhere in the room. Tell the players that the object of the game is to find the clock before the time runs out. At the signal word "tick," the players begin searching. When the signal "tock" is given, the players must freeze in place. The player who finds the clock yells "Ticktock!" If the alarm goes off before anyone finds the clock, the leader hides it again.

Table Football

Equipment:
- one paper triangle per team, approximately 2 inches (5 cm) in size
- tape
- a table or desk for each team

Where to Play:

at a table

Number of Players:

two

Directions:

Divide the players into pairs. Before the game begins, one player in each pair needs to fold a strip of paper into a right triangle and use tape to hold it together. This will be the football. One player places the football on the very edge of the table and flicks the long side of it with his or her fingers to the opposite end of the table. Each player has four tries to flick the football so that it leans over the opposite edge. This scores a touchdown. If the football falls off the edge, it becomes the other player's turn. If a player scores a touchdown, he or she gets six points and may try for an extra point. To score the point, his or her opponent forms a goal post with his or her hands. The other player stands the football on one end and tries to flick it up and through the goal post. If the kick is successful, the player earns one more point. The player with the most points after the time limit is the winner.

Chinese Hopscotch

Equipment:
- stones
- chalk
- a concrete area, divided into eight equal sections

Where to Play:
outdoors on concrete or blacktop

Number of Players:
two or more

Directions:
Before beginning this game, use chalk to draw a large, skinny rectangle. Divide the rectangle into eight equal squares and number them 1 through 8. The player kicks his or her stone into square 1. Then he or she hops all the way to square 8 on one foot. The player rests on both feet on square 8 before hopping back on the other foot to square 2. The player keeps going until he or she has kicked the stone all the way to square 8.

Chinese New Year's Day Game

Equipment:
- fortune cookies

Where to Play:

anywhere

Number of Players:

any number

Directions:

Distribute the fortune cookies and allow each player to share his or her fortune. Then have the players write fortunes for each other. After the fortunes are collected and distributed, the players spend time sharing and enjoying the funny predictions from their friends.

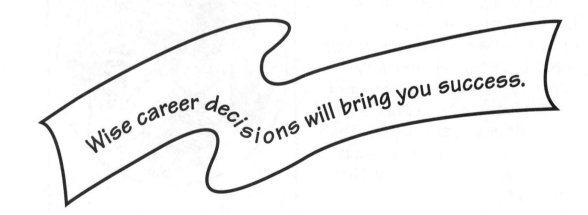

Wise career decisions will bring you success.

Friendship Circles

Equipment:
- large sheets of newsprint or poster paper
- tempera paint
- markers
- paper towels

Where to Play:

indoors

Number of Players:

any number

Directions:

This activity helps the players understand the principles that Martin Luther King, Jr. believed in and his dream for all people to join hands and be friends. Each player uses a marker to draw a large circle on his or her piece of paper. Then, every player, using a different color of paint, places a hand print on every other player's paper. The process is repeated until each player has formed a circle of hand prints.

I Have a Dream

Equipment:
- material on the life of Martin Luther King, Jr.
- a written or taped copy of the "I Have a Dream" speech
- paper
- pencils

Where to Play:

indoors

Number of Players:

any number

Directions:

The players listen to the "I Have a Dream" speech and share other materials on the topic. Each player brainstorms an idea for his or her own dream. The players write their basic ideas on small sheets of paper. One player collects the papers. He or she draws one piece of paper and then acts out the dream. The other players guess what the dream might be. The first player to guess correctly gets to draw and act out the next slip of paper.

"I Have A Dream"

Black History Trivia

Equipment:
- a library or reference books
- paper
- pencils

Where to Play:

indoors

Number of Players:

four or more

Directions:

Divide the players into teams. Give a copy of the questions on page 209 to each team. Give the teams 30 minutes or more to find as many answers as possible. The team with the most correct answers wins.

Black History Trivia *(cont.)*

1. Who is Harry Belafonte?

2. Did Mary McLeod Bethune work in the field of education?

3. Is Andrew Young the mayor of Chicago?

4. Who founded the NAACP?

5. What is slavery?

6. Where is Harlem?

7. What is an abolitionist?

8. What did Thurgood Marshall accomplish?

9. What is segregation?

10. Did blacks fight in the Civil War?

11. What sport did Arthur Ashe play?

12. What was the Emancipation Proclamation?

13. Who was Jackie Robinson?

14. Did Benjamin Booker establish a blood bank?

15. Were Matthew Henson and Estevanico both black explorers?

Presidential Picture Words

Equipment:

- a Lincoln hat, if available, or any container
- strips of paper
- pencil
- a chalkboard or a large easel with paper

Where to Play:

indoors

Number of Players:

four or more

Directions:

On strips of paper, write words that have to do with the presidents, such as *log cabin, cherry tree, election, Delaware,* etc. Divide the players into two teams. The players from each team take turns drawing a strip of paper from the hat. The player who draws a strip has one minute to draw a picture of the word or phrase while his or her teammates guess the word. If the team guesses correctly, they receive a point. The teams take turns until a predetermined amount of time has passed. When the time is up, the team with the most points wins the game.

Presidential Alphagories

Equipment:
- paper
- pencils

Where to Play:

indoors

Number of Players:

three or more

Directions:

Call out any letter of the alphabet. Give the players one minute to write as many words as possible beginning with that letter and having to do with presidents of the United States. Then repeat this process with another letter. You may wish to use more specific categories, such as birthplaces, first ladies, accomplishments, nicknames, etc. Or, you may select a certain president for each round. For example, if you choose Abraham Lincoln and the letter is L, the players might list liberty, log cabin, library, and lawyer. After each round give the players one point for each acceptable answer.

Heart Stopper

Equipment:
- music

Where to Play:

an open area

Number of Players:

any number

Directions:

While the music is playing, all of the players continuously dance and move. However, when the music stops, everyone is supposed to freeze in place. The leader may eliminate players who move after the music has stopped. The leader may use other tactics—suddenly changing tunes or tempos (faster music may make it harder for the players to stop quickly)—making someone laugh while the music is stopped—instructing the players to dance when the music is off—asking players to do things when the music is stopped—all in an attempt to fool the players into moving. The last player on the floor is the winner.

Valentine's Heart Game

Equipment:
- construction paper, preferably red or pink
- two dice

Where to Play:

indoors

Number of Players:

two or more

Directions:

Cut out 12 paper hearts, and write a message on one side of each one (such as, "Pretend you are a bird," "Cry like a baby," "Say something nice to a friend," "Tell a joke"). Number the hearts on their backsides and place them on the floor, message side down, in numerical order. The players take turns rolling the dice and turning over the heart that bears that number. The player must then act out the message on the heart card. To vary the game, more hearts and messages may be added.

Romantic Word Dictionary Race

Equipment:
- a dictionary for each player

Where to Play:

indoors

Number of Players:

two or more

Directions:

Call out one word at a time from the following list. The players race to look up the meanings of the words and use them in sentences.

sweetheart
beloved
lovingly
thoughtful
romance

cherished
fondly
endearment
affectionate
darling

adored
love
adorable
commitment
kindness

courtship
valentine
sentimental
tearful
enchantment

Happy Valentine's Day
Circle Tag

Equipment:
- none

Where to Play:

an open area

Number of Players:

five or more

Directions:

The players stand in a circle. One player volunteers to be "it" and walks around the outside of the circle. When "it" taps another player in the circle, he or she says "Happy Valentine's Day!" "It" continues walking while the tapped player simultaneously begins walking around the outside of the circle in the opposite direction. When the two players meet on the opposite side of the circle, they repeat "Happy Valentine's Day!" to each other, stop, and bow. The first player to return to the open place in the circle is safe, and the other player is "it" for the next round.

Irish Tag

Equipment:
- none

Where to Play:

an open area

Number of Players:

three or more

Directions:

In some games of tag, when a player tags another player the tagged player must place a hand on his or her part of the body that was tagged. He or she becomes "it" and must tag another player while keeping the hand in place. In this Irish "jig" version, every time a player is tagged, he or she must join hands, forming a chain. Chains and individuals may tag other chains and individuals until all of the players have been tagged and they create one long chain.

Lucky Storytellers

Equipment:
- paper
- pencils

Where to Play:

indoors

Number of Players:

two or more

Directions:

Divide the players into teams and give each team a list of some words related to St. Patrick's Day. Challenge the teams to each write a story, using all of the words, about someone who was lucky. Read the stories out loud for everyone to enjoy. Below is a sample list of words.

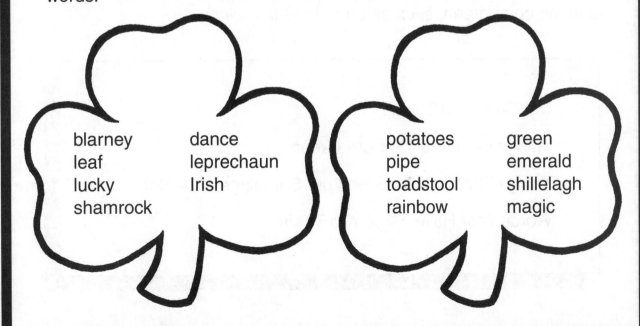

blarney   dance   potatoes   green
leaf   leprechaun   pipe   emerald
lucky   Irish   toadstool   shillelagh
shamrock   rainbow   magic

The Wearin' of the Green

Equipment:
- paper
- pencils

Where to Play:

anywhere

Number of Players:

any number

Directions:

Working individually or in groups, the players must list as many green things as possible in five minutes. When the five minutes are up, the players count their words, and the person with the most words wins. After the winner shares his or her words with the rest of the players, he or she may suggest another category related to St. Patrick's Day and the color green, such as one of the following:

Not-So-Green Things

Things in Nature That Are Green

Things That Can Be Green but Sometimes Are Not

Words That Have "Green" in Them

Snatch the Four-Leaf Clover

Equipment:
- a large, green shamrock made from construction paper

Where to Play:

an open area

Number of Players:

six or more

Directions:

Two teams line up facing each other about 20 to 30 feet (6 to 9 m) apart. They arrange themselves by height, with the shortest person on the right end of the line and the tallest on the left. The teams number off, starting at the right ends of their lines. The leader calls a number. Both players with that number try to snatch the four-leaf clover and return to his or her line without being tagged. The player that succeeds earns a point for his or her team. If the player is tagged, the other team receives a point. The leader then calls new numbers until all of the players have been called. The team with the most points wins the game.

1		8
2		7
3		6
4		5
5		4
6		3
7		2
8		1

Leprechaun Treasure Hunt

Equipment:
- treats or small prizes
- gold foil
- a small pot
- small, green construction paper shamrocks

Where to Play:

indoors or outdoors

Number of Players:

any number

Directions:

Hide the shamrocks and small pieces of gold foil throughout the play area before the game begins. Give the players 15 minutes to collect as much good luck (shamrocks) and riches (gold foil pieces) as they can. When the game is over, the players can trade their discoveries for small treats. As a variation, have the players name one thing that is green for every item that they find.

Touch the Magic Shamrock

Equipment:
- a green ball or other green object that is easy to catch
- candy or small treats (optional)

Where to Play:

an open area, indoors or outdoors

Number of Players:

five or more

Directions:

Have the players sit in a circle. Choose one player to be the leader. The leader starts the game by throwing the shamrock (green ball) to a player of his or her choice and then closes his or her eyes once the game gets underway. The first player must catch the shamrock and quickly toss it to another player. The game continues until the charm is tossed out of the circle. Then the last player to touch it should be the one to fetch it. After a short period, the leader shouts, "You're the lucky one!" The player who is holding the ball at this time leaves the circle and is given a small piece of candy. The game continues until all of the players are eliminated.

"You're the lucky one!"

Rainbow Toss

Equipment:
- poster board
- markers
- tape
- milk bottle caps (or coins if bottle caps are not available)
- a bowl

Where to Play:

at a table

Number of Players:

two to five

Directions:

Before the game begins, draw a large, colored rainbow on a piece of poster board. Tape it to one end of a table. Place the bottle caps (or coins) in a bowl at the other end of the table. The players take turns tossing caps or coins at the rainbow. They try to get one cap on each color or all of their caps on the same color. Create a point system for each of the different colors. The player with the most points after a predetermined period of time wins the game.

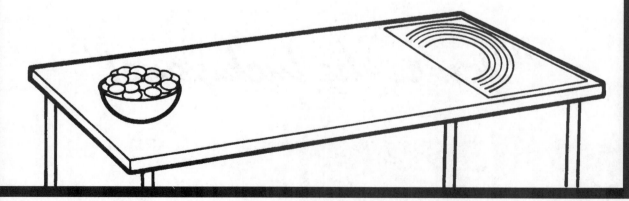

Two Truths and a Lie

Equipment:
- none

Where to Play:

anywhere

Number of Players:

two or more

Directions:

In this game, each player thinks of two interesting things about him- or herself that are true and one thing that is not true. He or she tells the three things to the group, and the group asks questions to determine which ones are the facts and which one is the lie. The players each guess which one is the lie, and then the truth is revealed. For example, a player may say "I once broke my arm, I have a twin sister, and I've ridden an elephant." The other players will ask questions like "How did you break your arm?" and "What's your sister's name?" It is the goal of the first player to fool the group.

I once broke my arm, I have a twin sister, and I've ridden an elephant.

How did you break your arm? What's your sister's name?

The Invisible Gift

Equipment:
 • none

Where to Play:
anywhere

Number of Players:
three or more

Directions:
The players form a circle (they may sit or stand). The first player secretly thinks of an object and must pretend to pass it to the next player in the circle. For instance, if he or she chooses a cat for the object, he or she could pretend to scoop it up, kiss it, pet it, and feed it a can of cat food. All of the actions must be done without speaking. The next player must pretend to take the item, indicate what it is without talking, and pass it to the next player. This continues until the last player receives the item. The last player announces to the group what he or she thinks the item is. If that player is wrong, the second-to-last player can take a guess, and so on. If no one guesses correctly, the first player reveals what the item is. The game continues with a new player choosing the item.

Fooled You!

Equipment:
- large pictures from books or magazines or posters

Where to Play:

anywhere

Number of Players:

any number

Directions:

Choose one player to be the leader. He or she holds up a picture from a book or magazine or a poster. The rest of the players are allowed to study it for one minute, and then they write everything that they remember seeing in the picture. The player with the most correct answers gets to display the next picture. As a variation, the leader can cover a picture of a single item, revealing only a small portion of it. The players are then asked to guess what the item is.

Airplane

Equipment:
- a large map
- blindfolds
- small paper airplanes
- pushpins or tape

Where to Play:

anywhere

Number of Players:

two or more

Directions:

This game is similar to the classic Pin the Tail on the Donkey game. Make a small paper airplane for each player. Attach a pushpin or a piece of tape to the nose of each one. Post the map on one wall, and line the players up at the opposite end of the room from the map. One by one, hand out the airplanes, blindfold the players, and point them toward the map. Each player must cross the room and place his or her airplane on the designated spot on the map, such as California, Iowa, etc. The player who reaches the map and pins his or her airplane closest to the designated spot is the winner.

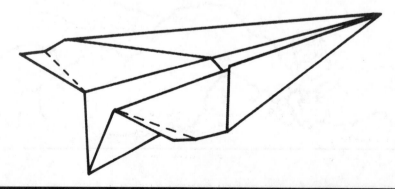

Blowing Game

Equipment:
- cotton ball or Ping-Pong ball
- small, lightweight objects
- medium-sized lid from a cardboard box
- scissors

Where to Play:

at a table

Number of Players:

two or more

Directions:

The object of this game is to experience how air affects objects of different weights and shapes. At the one end of a box lid, cut a hole which is large enough for a cotton ball or Ping-Pong ball to fall through. Place the lid right side up on the table in front of the player. The hole should be at the end farthest from the player's mouth. The players try to blow a number of objects (a pebble, piece of paper, a small leaf, a dime) across the lid and into the hole. For every object that the players drop through the hole, a point is earned.

Edible Map

Equipment:
- plain sugar cookie dough
- cookie sheets
- maps
- blue icing—for lakes and oceans
- green sprinkles—for plains
- clear or yellow sprinkles—deserts
- chocolate chips—mountains
- blue licorice—rivers
- candy-coated chocolate disks—capitals

Where to Play:
at a table

Number of Players:
any number

Directions:
Before beginning this activity, bake several large cookies in the shape of your state, the United States, or any other country or continent. Divide the players into groups and give each group a baked cookie to decorate. Encourage the groups to refer to their maps and to be as accurate as possible when decorating their cookies. When everyone has finished, have the groups share their maps. Each group may ask questions of the other players which can be answered by looking at the group's map. After the activity, the groups can enjoy eating their creations!

Geographical Twenty Questions

Equipment:
- a world map

Where to Play:

anywhere

Number of Players:

two or more

Directions:

This is a geographical version of the game Twenty Questions. The player who is "it" is supposed to think of a place on the map. The other players may ask questions about the place in the same manner as in Twenty Questions. When a player guesses the correct geographical location and then points to it on the map, he or she becomes "it" for the next round.

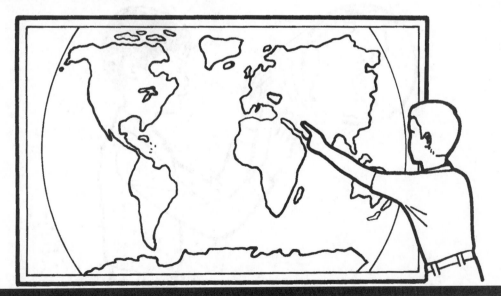

Toss the Globe

Equipment:
- a ball, decorated as a globe

Where to Play:

anywhere

Number of Players:

any number

Directions:

The first person starts the game by calling out the name of a place, and then he or she tosses the globe to one of the players. That player must locate the spot on the globe, call out another place, and then toss the globe to another player. If a player cannot locate the place before a predetermined time is up, he or she is out and must toss the globe to another player. The last person to remain in the game is the winner.

Mental Recycling

Equipment:
- pencils
- paper

Where to Play:

anywhere

Number of Players:

two or more

Directions:

Divide the participants into groups. Hand out the pencils and paper to the groups. Ask the players to brainstorm a list of new uses for all, or a selection, of the following items. Set a time limit. The group with the most ideas wins the game.

- an outdated globe
- an old telephone
- a leaky umbrella
- a book written in a language you do not know
- a venetian blind
- an aluminum can
- one water ski
- a stack of index cards
- a nonfunctioning computer keyboard

- an electric clock
- coffee filters
- a record collection
- a rundown flashlight battery
- a flat tire
- a dried-up ballpoint pen
- an empty juice box

Rabbit Relay

Equipment:
- one ball per team

Where to Play:

an open area

Number of Players:

six or more

Directions:

Divide the players into two relay teams. Determine a start line and a finish line. The team members must place the ball between their knees, hop to the finish line, and return to their relay team without dropping the ball. If the ball is dropped, the player must start over from the start line. When the first team members finish their part of the relay, they must hand off the balls to the next team players. The team which has all of its rabbits (players) finish first is the winner.

Spring Scavenger Hunt

Equipment:
- a list of objects found in nature
- small bags

Where to Play:

outdoors

Number of Players:

two or more

Directions:

Each player is given a list of things to find and a small container or bag to place them in. Give the players a certain amount of time in which to find as many of the items as possible. Some items on the list could be the following:

- a stone
- a leaf
- something that rolls
- a twig
- a white flower
- a yellow flower
- a seed
- something black and white

- a mud pie
- a blade of grass
- something smooth
- sand
- something made of wood
- a feather
- something shiny
- something that makes a noise

Hatching Eggs

Equipment:
- large construction paper eggs, cut into geometric shapes

Where to Play:

anywhere

Number of Players:

any number

Directions:

Give every player a construction paper egg. Challenge each player to arrange his or her egg pieces in a way that makes them look like a bird. Judge the birds in different categories such as most realistic and most creative.

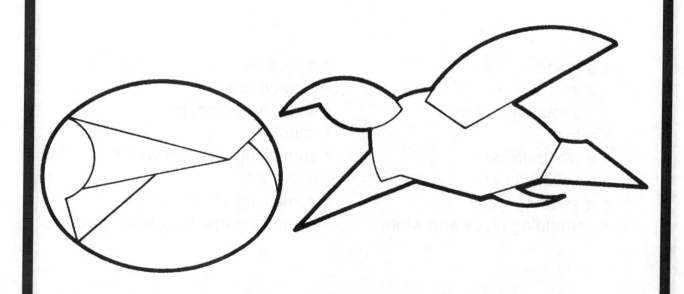

234

© Teacher Created Materials, Inc.

Egg and Spoon

Equipment:
- spoons
- hard-boiled eggs

Where to Play:

an open area

Number of Players:

four or more

Directions:

Give each player a spoon and an egg. Line up the players behind a start line. Whoever reaches the finish line first while balancing an egg on a spoon wins.

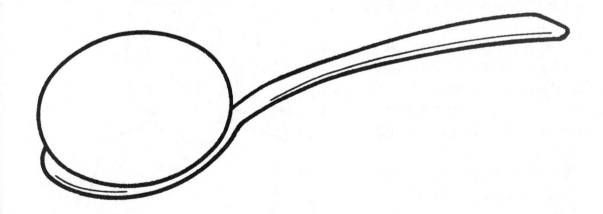

Easter Egg Obstacle Course

Equipment:
- an obstacle course
- hard-boiled eggs, one per player

Where to Play:

an open area

Number of Players:

two or more

Directions:

Before beginning the race, set up an obstacle course and explain it to the players. Different ways of walking through the course, such as crab-walking or walking backwards, may be expected. Give each player a hard-boiled egg. Every player must balance an egg on his or her head while maneuvering through the obstacle course. This may be played in teams as a relay or as a race among individuals. When finished, the players may want to color their eggs, make egg salad, or just eat them plain.

© Teacher Created Materials, Inc.

Cinco de Mayo Beanbag Toss

Equipment:
- five beanbags
- a Hula-Hoop
- a piñata
- a stick or broom handle

Where to Play:

an open area

Number of Players:

two or more

Directions:

Hang a Hula-Hoop (or other target with a hoop-like opening) from a tree or high place. Hang a piñata on another tree. The players take turns trying to toss the five beanbags through the Hoop. When a player succeeds at getting all five through the Hoop, he or she gets a turn at hitting the piñata. This continues until the piñata is broken and the candy falls out.

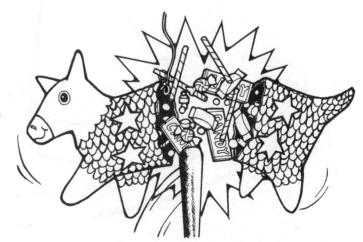

Cinco de Mayo Math Game

Equipment:
- blackboard or paper for displaying the directions
- paper
- pencils

Where to Play:

anywhere

Number of Players:

any number

Directions:

Have the players carefully complete each step on the next page.
(Hint: It makes this activity easier if the players put the numbers in order from smallest to largest first.)

(Answers to page 239: 1. 258; 2. 774; 3. 813; 4. 732; 5. 1,464; 6. 13,176; 7. 3,294; 8. 2781; 9. 1491; 10. 1871; 11. 1862)

Cinco de Mayo Math Game (cont.)

Using the following list of numbers, answer the questions:

27, 19, 2, 129, 9, 48

1. Multiply the largest number by the smallest.

2. Triple the answer for number 1.

3. Find the average of the six numbers. Add it to the answer for number 2.

4. Find the difference between the two largest numbers. Subtract it from the answer to number 3.

5. Double the answer to number 4.

6. Multiply the answer to number 5 by the second smallest number.

7. Double the smallest number, then divide it into the answer to number 6.

8. Multiply the third largest number by the fourth largest number. Subtract the product from the answer to number 7.

9. Multiply the largest number by 10. Subtract this product from the answer to number 8.

10. Multiply the third smallest number by 20. Add the product to the answer to number 9.

11. Subtract the second smallest number from the answer to number 10.

The year in Mexican history that Cinco de Mayo became an important day was_____.

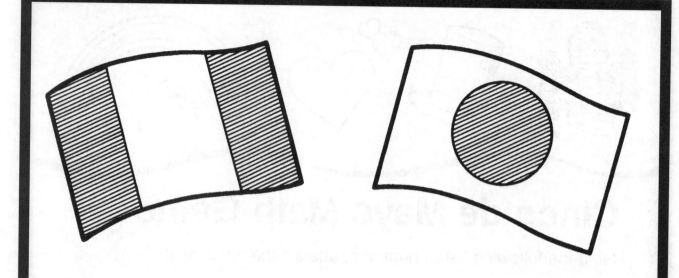

International Games

240   © Teacher Created Materials, Inc.

San Miguel's Circle—Mexico

Equipment:
- none

Where to Play:
indoors or outdoors

Number of Players:
at least four (however, this game works better with large numbers)

Directions:
This sing along game is a simple, impromptu activity. To begin, all of the players make a circle by holding hands and facing inward. The players then move clockwise and sing this rhyme:

> To San Miguel's Circle
> > they carry boxes of honey.
> To mellow, to mellow,
> > "[say a player's name] must turn around like a donkey!"

At the end of the rhyme, all of the players point to the player named in the rhyme, who must break from the circle, face outward, and then hold hands once again. This sequence continues until all of the players are facing outward. Then the game is rapidly concluded by all of the players moving backwards towards the center of the ring until they bump one another with their hips. At this point they all let go, clap, and laugh.

Risk Disk—United States

Equipment:
- 12-inch (30.4 cm) diameter cardboard disk, painted red on one side and white on the other

Where to Play:

a basketball court

Number of Players:

two teams of 5 to 15 players

Directions:

Choose one player to be the director who will take charge of the game. Have the teams line up in parallel lines approximately six yards (5.4 m) apart (or each three yards (2.7 m) away from the center line of the court). Use the end lines of the court as safe lines for the teams. Choose one team to be the red team and the other to be the white team. The director stands on a sideline centrally located between the two teams. The director then flips the disk into the air much like a giant coin toss. If it lands with the red side up, then the red team chases the white team to the white team's safe line. If the disk lands with its white side up, then the white team chases the red players. If a player is tagged before reaching his or her safe line, then he or she joins the opposite team. The game continues until one team has been completely tagged or when a predetermined number of rounds has been played.

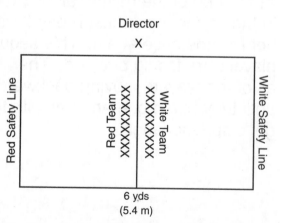

Bocce—Italy

Equipment:

- a regulation bocce set (nine balls of wood or solid rubber)
  (Note: Eight softballs and one hardball can be substituted for the regulation bocce set. Paint the hardball white and the softballs in two contrasting colors, for example, four red and four blue.)
- a coin

Where to Play:

outdoors (This game is traditionally played on a bordered field or alley measuring 8 x 60 feet (2.4 x 18.2 m). The alley contains a regulator peg in the center and foul areas at either end.)

Number of Players:

two to twelve

Directions:

The object of this game is to position your balls near the target ball, called the *pallino.* The game may be played by two individuals with two shots per turn or in teams of three to six with rotating turns of four shots each. Flip a coin to determine who brings the pallino into play. All of the balls, including the target ball, must be tossed from behind the foul line on the player's side. In order for the target ball to be considered in play, it must land at least five feet (1.5 m) beyond the regulator peg and out of any foul areas. Also, the target ball must be one foot (30.4 cm) or more from any sideline.

Bocce—Italy *(cont.)*

If the first attempt fails to land in play, then the teams alternate turns until the pallino is in a suitable position. Whoever is able to successfully position the target ball will have the first shot and begin the game. There are three types of throws a player may make: the straightforward bowl, the called shot, and the aerial shot. If a straightforward bowl disturbs any other ball, it is disqualified and the disturbed balls are repositioned. In a called shot, the thrown ball must hit a specified target or be disqualified (any disturbed balls on a disqualified shot will be repositioned). In the aerial shot, the target is called before the ball is thrown into the air; failure to hit the target will result in disqualification similar to the called shot. When all of the balls have been thrown, the score is computed. Each ball that is closer to the pallino than the opponent's best shot will score one point. Opposing balls measuring the same distance from the target ball will cancel one another from scoring. Victory is claimed upon reaching 15 points in a one-on-one game and 18 points for a team game.

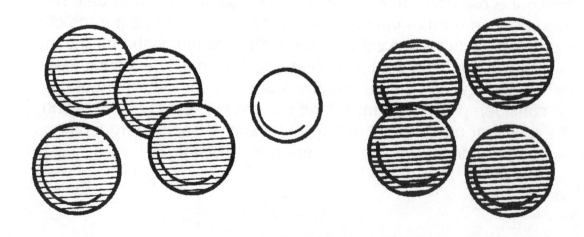

                    © *Teacher Created Materials, Inc.*

Kendo—Japan

Equipment:
- none

Where to Play:

indoors or outdoors

Number of Players:

14 or more

Directions:

Kendo is a game that pantomimes the fine art of Japanese fencing. Divide the players into pairs, and have each pair choose a leader. Scatter the pairs throughout the playing area. To begin the game, each pair starts to move around the playing area in a choo-choo train fashion. When two pairs meet face to face, the leader of each pair plays Rock, Paper, Scissors to decide which team will go first. Once the team order is decided, the two team leaders raise their arms overhead with their fists closed as if they are holding Japanese kendo swords. The lead player from the first team screams "Hee-Yah!," steps forward, and strikes one of the following three poses while shouting its name: **Men** *(face mask)*—hands on top of head; **Do** *(chest plate)*—hands on hips; **Kote** *(arm guards)*—right hand grasps left forearm. The leader of the second team simultaneously strikes another pose while shouting its name. If this pose is different from the lead player's pose, then the roles reverse and the game continues. If the pose is the same as that of the lead player, then the opposing player loses and moves behind his or her partner. The battle continues until both players in one of the pairs have been defeated. At this time, the pairs resume their moving around the playing area in search of another pair to battle.

Ojiisan-Obaasan—Japan

Equipment:
- two blindfolds
- a gong or bell

Where to Play:

indoors or outdoors

Number of Players:

10 to 30

Directions:

Arrange the players in a large circle, facing inward with a distance of three to four feet (.91–1.2 m) between their outstretched arms. This formation will create the playing area and its boundaries. Select two volunteers (preferably one male and one female) to stand in the center of the circle. Give them the titles of *ojiisan* (grandfather) and *obaasan* (grandmother). Blindfold one of the players and give the bell to the other player. Turn the blindfolded player around two to three times to disorient him or her. The blindfolded player then calls to the other player "obaasan, obaasan" or "ojiisan, ojiisan." Each time the player with the bell is called, he or she must ring the bell. The blindfolded player tries to find and tag the bell ringer while the bell ringer avoids being tagged. Neither player may leave the boundaries of the circle. Once the bell ringer is tagged, the two players may reverse roles, or two new individuals may be chosen to be obaasan and ojiisan. To make this game more challenging, both volunteers may be blindfolded. In this case, the players comprising the circle must gently redirect them towards the center if they start to leave the playing area.

 © Teacher Created Materials, Inc.

Yoté—West Africa

Equipment:
- 12 pebbles
- 12 sticks

Where to Play:

outdoors

Number of Players:

two

Directions:

Create a Yoté board by digging 30 small holes (six columns and five rows) into the dirt or sand. Each player begins with 12 markers. One player uses pebbles, and the other player uses small pieces of stick. The game begins when the holder of the rocks places one rock into any hole. The stick player then places a stick into any open hole. Only one marker may be played per turn. A player is not required to put all of his or her markers on the board before moving the previously positioned markers around the Yoté board. At any time a player may choose to move one of his or her previously placed markers. These markers may only move one space up, down, left, or right and only into an empty hole. A player may capture an opposing marker (remove it from play) by passing a marker over it and into an empty hole. The capturing player is then allowed a bonus capture, removing from play an additional opposing marker from the board. The winner is the first player to capture all of his or her opponent's markers. However, the game may be called a draw if both players have three or fewer markers remaining on the board.

Dreidel—Israel

Equipment:
- a dreidel (handmade or purchased)
- tokens

Where to Play:

indoors or outdoors

Number of Players:

two or more

Directions:

Have the players form a circle. Give each player an equal number of tokens or coins with which to play. Each player contributes two tokens to the pot before the game begins. Choose who will spin the dreidel first. Each player will spin the dreidel on his or her turn and score in the following manner:

The player takes the center pile.

Gimmel

The player must give half.

Shin

The player does nothing.

Nun

The player receives half of the pile.

Hay

This game can also be played in the following manner. All of the players alternate spinning the dreidel until the "G" faces upright subsequent to spinning. The player who spins the "G" is the winner and scores one point. The person with the highest points after 10 rounds is the winner.

          © *Teacher Created Materials, Inc.*

Dreidel—Israel *(cont.)*

Dreidel Pattern:

A dreidel is a top with four flat sides with the initials N, G, H, and S marked on its sides. These letters represent the Hebrew message "nes gadol hayah sham" or "a great miracle happened there."

Dreidel Directions:

Cut out the dreidel. Make holes on the top and bottom. Fold along the inside lines to make a box. Use glue or tape to hold it together. Push a pencil or pen through the holes. Spin the dreidel, and begin the game.

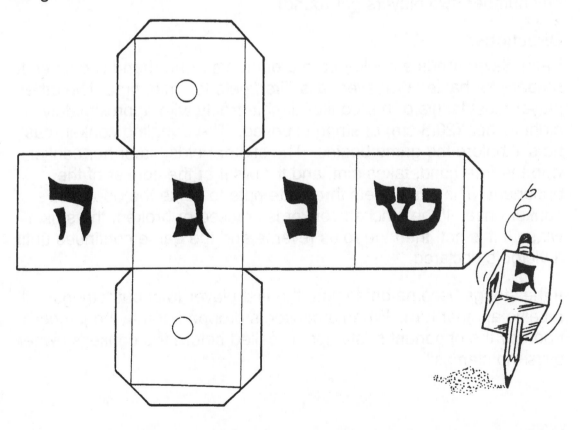

Conkers—England, Scotland, Australia

Equipment:
- handmade conkers (see next page)
- strong cording

Where to Play:

indoors or outdoors

Number of Players:

any number (two players per round)

Directions:

Each player winds a conker cord around his or her hand two times to prepare for battle. Whoever calls "first" gets to strike first. The other player must let his or her conker dangle freely with approximately eight inches (20.3 cm) of string exposed. The dangling conker must be still before the game begins. The striker holds his or her conker with the free hand, takes aim, and throws it at the conker of the opponent. The striker gets three attempts to strike the opponent's conker once. If the stricken conker is cracked or broken, the striker wins. If it is not, then the roles reverse and the game continues until a victor is declared.

If the strings become entangled, the first player to shout "strings" will receive another turn. When a conker is dropped, it may be jumped upon by the opponent if "stamps" is called before the conker's owner says "no stamps!"

250 © Teacher Created Materials, Inc.

Conkers—England, Scotland, Australia *(cont.)*

A conker which is stamped upon is considered defeated by the stamper. With each victory a conker is labeled with a new rank and name—"oner" for defeating one opponent, "twoer" for defeating two, and so on. Conkers also acquire the rankings of the conkers they defeat, for example, if a "sevener" beats a "twoer," it becomes a "niner."

How to Make a Conker:

Before beginning the game, prepare a conker for every player. Choose hard round nuts such as walnuts, chestnuts, hazelnuts, or acorns, and drill a hole clear through the center of each one. String each nut onto a piece of cord, and tie knots on the ends to prohibit the nut from sliding off the cord.

"Strings"

"no stamps"

"Stamps"

"Sevener" + "twoer" = "niner"

Hoops—Greece

Equipment:
- a hoop of plastic, rubber, or an inflated tire tube for each player
- a stick for bowling (rolling) for each player

Where to Play:

outdoors

Number of Players:

one or more

Directions:

Hoop rolling has been a form of exercise for many years. Historically, there are references to it dating back to Ancient Greece (300 B.C.). To begin this modern version of the game, a player holds the hoop with one hand, fingers pointed downward. The player then bends slightly and flings the hoop forward. He or she runs after the hoop and tries to keep it rolling with one hand or a stick. Once two or more individuals have mastered hoop rolling, then a variety of games may be played. Try Hoop Haces, Hoop Relays, Hoop Targets, Follow the Hoop Leader, etc. If the hoop is big enough, the player may even try to jump through it while it is rolling.

Quoits—Scotland, England

Equipment:
- four 6-inch (15.2 cm) quoits (rings)
- one or more hobs (upright poles)

Where to Play:

outdoors

Number of Players:

two or four players

Directions:

Quoits is similar to the American game of horseshoes and dates back to the fourteenth century. Historically, two clay beds stood 18 yards (16.46 m) apart. In the middle of the bed stood an iron hob or pole. The players alternated turns. The object was to throw the rings over the hob and, in doing so, earn points for the team.

Quoits may be made out of . . .
- garden hose of $\frac{1}{2}$-inch (1.2 cm) diameter cut into 18–20 inch (45.7–50.8 cm) pieces and connected with wooden dowel joiners and electrician's tape.
- rope of $\frac{1}{2}$-inch (1.2 cm) diameter cut into 18–20 inch (45.7–50.8 cm) pieces and connected with electrician's tape
- aluminum or copper wire cut into 18–20 inch (45.7–50.8) pieces and formed into circles.

Quoits—Scotland, England *(cont.)*

Hobs may be made out of . . .

- metal rods hammered into the soil.
- wooden dowels mounted onto wooden bases.

Scoring differentials are made by changing the number of hobs and/or height of the hobs. The players stand together 6 yards (5.49 m) from the hob bed and take turns throwing at the hobs. All of the points earned per round are added into the cumulative totals. If two quoits land around the same hob, they cancel out each other's point. The first player or team to total 21 points is the winner.

Prooi—Holland

Equipment:
- none

Where to Play:

indoors

Number of Players:

10 to 30 (recommended for ages six and above)

Directions:

The game of Prooi (pronounced "proy") should be played in a room big enough for all of the players to roam around in without getting hurt or lost. Turn off the lights or have the players close their eyes as they move around. Secretly choose one player to be the prooi; none of the other players should know his or her identity. When the lights go off, each player explores the room with his or her arms extended in search of one another. It is important that they continue to move until they meet someone else. When a player stumbles upon another player, he or she will ask "Prooi?" The prooi will say nothing, grasp the inquiring player's hand, and the two will stay silently together. If the encountered player is not the prooi, he or she will respond by saying "Prooi." Then both players will continue exploring the room. As time goes by, the room will quiet down as more and more people discover and join the prooi. Eventually, the game will end when all of the players have found the prooi or when a predetermined amount of time has passed.

Lummi Sticks—New Zealand

Equipment:
- two lummi sticks per player (wooden dowels approximately 18 inches (45.7 cm) long and 1 inch (2.54 cm) in diameter)

Where to Play:

indoors or outdoors

Number of Players:

any even number

Directions:

Divide the players into pairs. Have the pairs sit cross-legged on the ground facing each other. The distance between the coupled players should allow for an easy exchange of the lummi sticks (approximately one foot [30.48 cm] with arms extended forward). If all of the players will be chanting the song in unison, have them sit fairly close together; otherwise, let the pairs scatter around the playing area. The players begin the game with a lummi stick in each hand, held perpendicularly about 6 inches (15.24 cm) from the ground. The partners perform the following sequence:

1. Hold the sticks vertically, and tap the bottoms to the ground—tap the sticks together—tap the right stick to the partner's right stick—tap the stick bottoms to the ground—tap together—tap the left stick to the partner's left stick.

2. Hold the sticks vertically, and tap the stick bottoms to the ground—tap the sticks together—tap the right stick to the partner's right stick, and then tap the left stick to the partner's left stick—tap the ground—tap together—tap the partner's right stick with the right stick—tap the partner's left stick with the left stick.

Lummi Sticks—
New Zealand *(cont.)*

3. Tap the stick bottoms to the ground—tap together—tap both sticks simultaneously with the partner's two sticks (one player's sticks go inside while the other player's sticks go outside)—tap the bottoms to the ground—tap together—tap the partner's sticks.

4. Repeat patterns 1 through 3. However, instead of tapping each other's sticks, exchange lummi sticks by tossing the stick or sticks to one another. Toss the lummi sticks forward and slightly upwards so the stick is vertical. Decide in advance whose stick(s) will take the inside path and whose will take the outside path.

5. Tap the stick bottoms to the ground—tap together—toss the left-hand stick into the right hand while the right-hand stick is tossed to the partner's left hand—continue this square-patterned stick exchange for 15 more beats.

6. Extend the right arm out to the side with the lummi stick held horizontally by the bottom, and tap the tip to the ground—flip the stick and catch it by its other end—tap the tip to the ground— extend the left arm out, holding the stick in a similar fashion, and tap the tip to the ground—flip the stick—tap the tip to the ground—extend both arms forward, and tap both of the tips to the ground—flip the sticks—tap the tips to the ground—hold the sticks vertically, and tap the bottoms to the ground—tap

Lummi Sticks— New Zealand *(cont.)*

together—toss the right-hand stick to the partner's right hand—extend the left arm out to the side with the lummi stick held horizontally at the bottom, and tap the tip to the ground—flip the stick and catch it by its other end—tap the tip to the ground—extend the right arm out, holding the stick in similar fashion, and tap the tip to the ground—flip the stick—tap the tip to the ground—extend both arms forward, and tap both of the tips to the ground—flip the sticks—tap the tips to the ground—hold the sticks vertically, and tap the bottoms to the ground—tap together—toss the left-hand stick to the partner's left hand.

258

© Teacher Created Materials, Inc.

Lummi Sticks— New Zealand *(cont.)*

7. Extend both arms to the sides, holding the horizontal sticks by the bottoms—tap the tips to the ground—flip the sticks, catching them by their other tips—tap the tips to the ground twice—flip the sticks in one complete circle, catching them by their original ends—tap the tips to the ground—hold the sticks vertically, and tap the bottoms to the ground—tap the sticks together—toss the right-hand stick to the partner's right hand—tap the bottoms to the ground—tap together—toss the left-hand stick to the partner's left hand—repeat this entire sequence.

Each sequence is performed at three-quarter time to the following chant:

> **"Ma-ku-ay/Ko-ta-o/We-ku-e/Tan-o/Ma-ku-ay/Ko-ta-o/We-ku e/Tan-o."**

If performed properly, each step will finish with the song.

Snake in the Grass—India

Equipment:
- none

Where to Play:

indoors or outdoors

Number of Players:

10 or more

Directions:

Determine the playing field boundaries according to the size of the group. Choose one person to be the snake. The snake gets down on his or her hands and knees in a steady, unmoving position. At the start of the game, all of the other players must gather around the snake and touch the snake or be linked through the touch of another player (in a chain-like fashion) to the snake. After a predetermined countdown, the snake comes to life and attempts to strike the other players by touching them. The touched players also turn into snakes. The game continues until all of the players become snakes. The last player to be touched begins the next game as the snake.

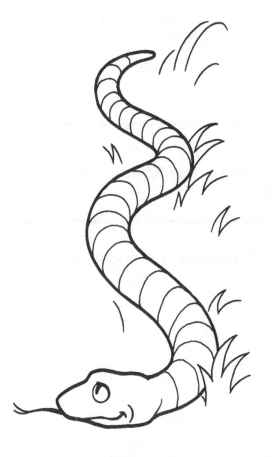

Speedball—United States

Equipment:
- a soccer ball or a small basketball
- pennants or jerseys are recommended to identify teams
- a coin

Where to Play:

outdoors on a regulation football field

Number of Players:

preferably two teams of 11 (However, any number of players may constitute a team. If the teams are really small, the game can be played on one-half of a football field [widthwise] with the goals placed 10 yards [9.1 m] beyond the sidelines.)

Directions:

Divide the players into two teams, and ask the teams to choose heads or tails for a coin toss. The winner of the coin toss has the choice of kicking, receiving, or defending a specific goal. The loser of the coin toss has the same choice at the beginning of the second half of the game. The game is started with a kickoff from the kicking team's own 50-yard line. Both teams are required to remain behind the field's center line until the ball is kicked. The receiving team's players attempt to move the ball downfield and score by kicking, passing, or bouncing the ball off of their bodies.

Speedball—United States *(cont.)*

Running with the ball is not allowed, and there is no tackling or interference. If a team causes the ball to go out of bounds, a throw-in (any style) is given to the opposing team. If the ball goes over the end line without scoring, the ball is given to the opposing team who may pass or kick the ball from out of bounds at that point. In the case that two or more players are contesting possession of the ball, a tie will be declared, action will stop, and the ball will be tossed up between them to resume play again. The most characteristic features of speedball are the rules regarding the playing privileges of aerial balls and ground balls.

The following rules apply:

Kickoff: A kickoff is made by a place kick on or behind the 50-yard line. The kicking team must remain behind the ball until it is kicked, and the receiving team must remain behind the center line until the ball is kicked. The ball must travel 10 yards (9.1m) before the kickers may touch it unless it is touched by the receivers first. If the ball is kicked out of bounds, it goes to the opponents. If the ball is touched, but not propelled out of bounds, the ball goes to the receiver(s) closest to where the ball went out. If it is touched but is propelled by one or more receivers out of bounds, it goes to the kickers. A field goal from kickoff receives three points.

Aerial or Fly Ball: A ball that has been clearly raised into the air by a hand, foot, or other body part remains a fly ball until it again hits the ground. A fly ball may be caught, held, passed, punted, drop-kicked, or otherwise played by the body.

Speedball—United States *(cont.)*

Ground Ball: A ground ball may be stationary, rolling, or bouncing. Even if it is in the air subsequent to a bounce, it is ruled as a ground ball. Kicking, heading, and bouncing the ball off of the body are the only means allowed for playing a ground ball.

Passing: The ball may be passed in any direction to any player or advanced by one overhead dribble which the passer may catch himself or herself. However, in any instance, a player may not handle the ball with his or her hands unless it is received as a fly ball.

Kicking: A ball in play may be punted, drop-kicked, dribbled, or juggled with the feet. A loose fly ball may not be kicked.

Dribbling of the Ball: The players may dribble the ball with the feet. They may bat or tap a fly ball or drop a caught fly ball to the ground and play it as a drop-kick or a kicking dribble. The players may use one overhead dribble to advance the ball without the aid of teammates. However, they may not score a touchdown by this method.

Traveling: A player who is standing still while catching a ball may take one step in any direction but must get rid of the ball before completing a second step. If running, the player is allowed two steps. If at full speed, it is the referee's judgment to decide if the player stopped as soon as possible. A player may not step over the goal line to score. It is a violation to travel, or carry the ball, more than the allotted steps.

Speedball—United States *(cont.)*

Tie Ball: A tie ball occurs when the ball is held simultaneously by two players or when the referee is in doubt as to who has possession. When a tie ball is declared, play stops. A tipoff is conducted between the two players in order to resume play. A tipoff may not directly result in a score. A tie ball is used at center field, following double fouls, and at the start of overtime periods.

Goaltenders: There is no distinction made between the goaltender and the other players regarding restrictions and privileges of playing the ball.

Defensive Play: A player may legally guard an opponent who has the ball. Opponents must play to secure the ball and in no way grab or hold the opposing players.

Fouls, Personal: Kicking, tripping, charging, pushing, holding, blocking, and unnecessary roughness of any kind (such as running into another player from behind or kicking at a fly ball and thereby hitting an opponent) are all considered personal fouls. Four personal fouls will disqualify a player from the game.

Fouls, Technical: Illegal substitution, more than three time-outs in a game, unsportsmanlike conduct, and unnecessarily delaying the game are all considered technical fouls.

 © Teacher Created Materials, Inc.

Speedball—United States *(cont.)*

Violation: Traveling with the ball, using hands or arms on a ground ball, a double overhead dribble, violating a tie ball, and kicking or kneeing a fly ball before catching it (if it results in kicking an opponent, then it is a personal foul) are all considered violations.

Penalties: The offended player will be granted a penalty kick or possession of the ball as follows:

- A personal foul in the field of play . . . one penalty kick with no follow-up.

- A technical foul in the field of play . . . one penalty kick with no follow-up.

- A violation in the field of play . . . out-of-bounds ball given to the opponent.

- A personal foul in the end zone . . . two penalty kicks with follow-up on the last.

- A technical foul in the end zone . . . one penalty kick with follow-up.

- A violation in the end zone . . . one penalty kick with follow-up.

Speedball—United States *(cont.)*

Summary of Fouls: Fouls in the field of play allow for no follow-up; whereas, fouls in the end zone will always allow for at least one follow-up. On penalty kicks with follow-up, the kicking side is behind the ball and the defending side is behind the end line or in the field of play. No one is allowed between the goalposts except for a goalkeeper. The penalty kicker may not play the ball again until after another player plays it, and he or she must make an actual attempt at a goal.

Timing: The game is comprised of four, 10-minute quarters, with a two-minute rest in between. There is a 10-minute break between the halves. Five-minute periods are granted in the case of overtime play.

Time-Outs: Three legal time-outs of two minutes each are permitted during the game. Substitutions may be made at any time when the ball is not in play. If a player is withdrawn, he or she may not return during that same period.

Scoring Methods:

- Field Goal (3 points): A field goal is achieved by a soccer-type kick in which a ground ball is kicked under the crossbar and between the goalposts from the field of play or end zone. (A punt going straight through is not a field goal because it is not a ground ball. The ball must hit the ground first.)

- Drop-Kick (1 point): A drop-kick must be made from the field of play and go over the crossbar and between the uprights.

 © Teacher Created Materials, Inc.

Speedball—United States *(cont.)*

- End Goal (1 point): An end goal is a ground ball, kicked or legally bodied from any player from the end zone, which passes over the end line but not between the goalposts.

- Penalty Kick (1 point): A penalty kick is a ball kicked from the penalty mark that goes under the crossbar and between the goalposts. The penalty mark is placed directly in front of the goal, along the goal line.

- Touchdown (2 points): A touchdown is a forward pass completed from the field of play into the end zone. The player must have both feet within the end zone; otherwise, the play will continue without a score. If the player is outside of the sidelines or over the end line, the ball is out of bounds. If the forward pass is missed or dropped, the play continues; however, the ball must return to the field of play before a forward pass or drop-kick may be attempted.

Variation: Speedball may be played by adding an element of touch football. A player in possession of the ball may run with the ball until tagged by an opponent. A touchdown may be scored by carrying the ball over the goal line. If a player is tagged while carrying the ball, then he or she forfeits the ball to his or her opponent, and the ball is brought into play from out of bounds.

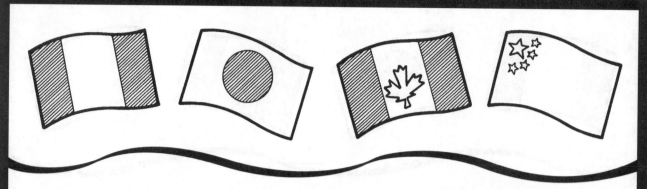

European Handball—Denmark

Equipment:
- a ball which is slightly smaller than a standard soccer ball
- pennants or jerseys are recommended to identify teams

Where to Play:

outdoors on a rectangular playing field, approximately 60 x 120 feet (18.2 x 36.5 m) in size

Number of Players:

two teams of seven (This may be increased, based upon the overall age and experience of the players.)

Directions:

Set up the playing field as shown in the diagram below. Include two goal areas, free-throw lines, penalty lines, and a center line. In the middle of each goal line, add a goal measuring 10 feet wide (3 m) and six feet (1.8 m) high.

Divide the players into two teams. Before starting the game, toss a coin to decide which player will place the ball into play or choose a goal to defend. The ball is placed into play by a team member throwing the ball in from out of bounds, next to the centerline. The players try to move the ball downfield in an attempt to throw the ball past the opposing goalie and into the opponent's goal. As soon as a team member gets the ball, he or she should attempt to move the ball down the field before the defense can set up.

European Handball—Denmark

(cont.)

Most scoring is made from leaping into the air and throwing from above. The most effective throws are made while jumping into the goal area but letting go of the ball before to making ground contact within the goal area. One point is scored for each goal made.

After a score, the non-scoring team will have a throw-in from out of bounds next to the centerline in order to resume play of the game. The game is divided into two halves of approximately 15 minutes each. The teams switch goals and direction of play after the first half. The time clock will stop after goals or violations of play. The time clock resumes when the ball is brought back into play.

The following rules apply:

Time-Outs: Time-outs are only allowed for injuries or substitutions. Substitutions may only be made when the ball is out of play.

Area Restrictions: The goal area is restricted to the goalie's use; no other player may enter the goal area to play the ball. Both teams' players must be in their own respective halves of the field when the ball is put into play at the start of the game or after a goal. Once the ball is placed into play, all of the players may move freely around the playing field.

Throwing and Catching: The ball may be handled by any part of the body above the knees. Accidental contact below the knees is acceptable, but no ball control is permitted. The ball may be held by a player for no more than three seconds. A player may take only three steps while in possession of the ball. A player may choose to bounce the ball and catch it with both hands in order to advance the ball; the limitation on steps does not apply during the bounce.

European Handball—Denmark

(cont.)

Guarding and Ball Recovery: Only one hand may be used while playing a ball which is another player's possession. The hand must be kept in an open palmed fashion, and no tie-ups or ball stealing are allowed. Blocking, pushing, tripping, holding, or other forms of unnecessary roughness while guarding another player are not permitted. Except for the use of the bounce, a player may not pass the ball to himself or herself.

The Goalie: Goalies may use any body part to block the ball. If the ball enters the goal area or touches the goalie or the goal line, it belongs to the goalie (as long as it does not roll back into the playing area). The goalie is not restricted by handling time or number of steps he or she may take. The goalie should put the ball back into play quickly, or he or she will receive a penalty for unsportsmanlike conduct. The goalie may not leave the goal area with the ball or bring the ball back into the safety of the goal area. Once the goalie enters the playing field, he or she is no longer protected by the rights of a goalie until returning to the goalie area. When in the playing field area, the goalie may throw the ball into play, but he or she may not kick it.

Throw-In: Throw-ins are done at the start of the game, after a goal, and after the ball goes out of bounds. An out-of-bounds throw-in is performed from the sideline adjacent to where the ball went out of bounds. Goals may not be made directly from the throw-in. Throw-ins are to be performed in a two-hand, overhead method similar to that used in soccer.

European Handball—Denmark

(cont.)

Corner Throw-In: A corner throw-in is used when the ball was last touched by the defenders prior to rolling over their goal line. The corner throw-in is done from the corner and may be thrown in any manner to put the ball into play.

Free Throw: Free throws are given to the opposing team whenever the following infractions occur: traveling more than three steps, holding the ball for more than three seconds, offsides, illegal entering of the goal area, illegal guarding, or playing the ball with the feet. A free throw is given from the spot where the infraction was made except when the infraction happened between the goal line and the free throw line; then it is performed from the free throw line. All of the defenders must stand at least 10 feet away from the spot of the free throw. If the free throw is given to the offensive team at the free throw line, then all of the defenders stand in front of the goal area boundary.

Penalty Shot: Penalty shots are given for rough play, entering the goal area to block an attempt, intentional throwing of a ball into the goal area by a defender, the goalie bringing the ball into the playing field, pushing a player into the goal area, or any other unsportsmanlike conduct. A penalty shot is taken at the penalty line with only the goalie defending the goal. All of the other players must remain behind the free-throw line. If the goal is missed, the ball is considered to be in play and the game resumes.

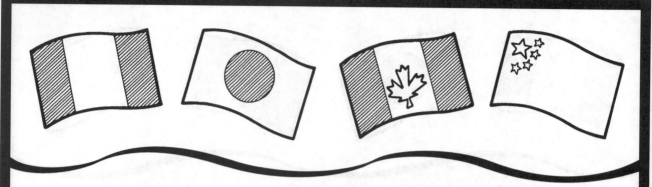

Indian Kickball—Mexico (Tarahumara Indians)

Equipment:
- two kickballs (This game is traditionally played with two rubber balls approximately three inches [7.6 cm] in diameter.)

Where to Play:
outdoors

Number of Players:
six to twelve players

Directions:
Divide the players into two teams. Give each team its own kickball. Mark the balls ahead of time so that they are easily distinguishable from one another. Create a long racecourse. This game is traditionally played on a racecourse of about a mile or so with plenty of changes in direction; however, it can be adapted to fit your needs. Be sure to include clearly marked start and finish lines. The two teams should gather at the start line, each surrounding their team ball. Separate the teams by five to ten yards (4.5 to 9.1 m). Give a starting signal to begin the race. The first team member for each team delivers a lifting kick, and the other team members chase after the ball in the hopes of advancing the ball along the racecourse in a similar manner. All of the team members need to stay close to each other and the ball, functioning as a single entity. The first team to cross the finish line with its ball wins.

272

© Teacher Created Materials, Inc.

Pelele—Spain

Equipment:
- a blanket
- a homemade dummy (see the next page) or a stuffed animal

Where to Play:

outdoors or an indoor area with a very high ceiling

Number of Players:

three or more

Directions:

The players lay the blanket on the floor and place the dummy in the center of the blanket. Each player then takes a sturdy grip of the edge of the blanket. At a given signal, all of the players lift the blanket and throw the dummy high into the air. Each time the dummy comes back down, the players catch it in the blanket and throw the dummy back up again. The players attempt to get the dummy higher and higher with each throw. Often the players will sing a song while tossing the dummy. The following song may be used.

Pelele, Pelele,
Tu madre te quiere,
Tu padre tambien,
Todos te queremos.
Arriba con el!

Pelele, Pelele,
Your mother loves you,
And your father too,
We all love you.
Up with him!

Pelele—Spain *(cont.)*

How to Make Your Own Dummy:

1. Stuff a pair of socks with straw and sew them shut.

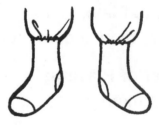

2. Insert the socks into two trouser legs and secure them with a strong thread.

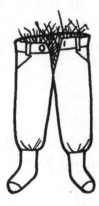

3. Stuff the trouser legs with straw, packing them snugly.

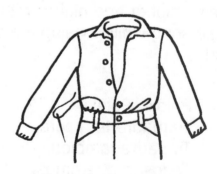

4. Sew shut the sleeves of a shirt and sew the bottom of the shirt inside the trouser waistband.

Pelele—Spain *(cont.)*

How to Make Your Own Dummy *(cont.)*:

5. Stuff the shirt with straw.

6. Fill a flour sack or a small pillowcase with straw, and securely sew it into the shirt collar.

7. Paint a face on your dummy, and attach a wig.

8. Add a nose or ears by stuffing small pockets of cloth and sewing them onto the dummy's head.

To the Viper—Mexico

Equipment:
- none

Where to Play:

indoors or outdoors

Number of Players:

at least four (However, this game works better with large numbers.)

Directions:

Choose two volunteers to create an arch by holding hands and raising them over their heads. Name one volunteer "cantaloupe" and the other one "watermelon." The rest of the players parade single file under the arch while the two volunteers chant:

> To the viper, to the viper, of the sea,
>
> through here one child wishes to pass.
>
> Which one will it be?
>
> The one in front or the one behind?
>
> The one in front runs too fast,
>
> the one behind shall remain.

Upon saying the word "remain" the arch lowers and traps a player. The two volunteers then ask the imprisoned player "Which do you wish to be, cantaloupe or watermelon?" The player then lines up behind the person he or she has chosen. After all of the players have been trapped and have joined a side, each player will hold on to the waist of the child lined up in front of him or her. The two chains then pull the arch until it breaks. The team with the most children on its side is the winner.

Doña Blanca—Mexico

Equipment:

Where to Play:

indoors or outdoors

Number of Players:

at least six (However, this game works better with large numbers.)

Directions:

Have the players form a circle by holding hands and facing inward. Choose a volunteer to stand in the center of the circle and play the beautiful Doña Blanca. Then choose a second volunteer to stand outside of the circle and play the evil rogue. It is the goal of the rogue to catch Doña Blanca while the entire group follows this script.

All:	Doña Blanca is covered with gold and silver pillars.
The Rogue:	We will break a pillar to see Doña Blanca.
All:	Who is the person who is after Doña Blanca?
The Rogue:	I am the person after Doña Blanca! Where is Doña Blanca?
All:	She went to church.
The Rogue:	Bad luck and dress shirts! (The player leaves and then returns.) Where is Doña Blanca?
All:	She went to the square.
The Rogue:	Bad luck and pumpkins! (The player leaves and then returns.) Where is Doña Blanca?

Doña Blanca—Mexico *(cont.)*

All: She went to the hill.

The Rogue: Bad luck and calves! (The player leaves and then returns.) Where is Doña Blanca?

All: She has arrived!

(Now the Rogue tries to capture Doña Blanca by performing the following: He or she touches a player in the circle and asks . . .)

The Rogue: What is the pillar made of?

All: Gold! (Then the rogue moves on to another player and asks . . .)

The Rogue: What is the pillar made of?

All: Silver!

This play continues around the circle. The rogue may hear answers such as marble, iron, lead, plaster, brick, wax, and straw. Upon the answer "straw," the circle breaks open. The rogue enters inside while Doña Blanca flees, protected by the new wall. When the rogue finally catches Doña Blanca, new roles are chosen.

Juan Pirulero—Mexico

Equipment:
- none

Where to Play:

indoors or outdoors

Number of Players:

at least four (However, this game works better with larger numbers.)

Directions:

Have the players form a circle. Choose one player to be the director and stand in the center of the circle. Every player will choose a trade whose characteristic movements he or she will pantomime while the director pretends to play a clarinet. The players need to pay very close attention, because whenever the director imitates the movements of another player's trade, everyone else must change his or her pantomime to match that of the director. If a player is distracted and fails to do so, then he or she will give a pledge to the group to perform a silly act or deed after the game. To begin the first and all subsequent rounds of the game, this chant is recited by all of the players:

> *"This is the game of Juan Pirulero; see that everyone is paying attention!"*

Shuttlecock—China, Japan, Korea

Equipment:
- shuttlecock (see below)

Where to Play:

outdoors

Number of Players:

one or more

Directions:

Give each player a shuttlecock (handmade or store bought). When playing alone the object is to keep the shuttlecock aloft. Begin by tossing the shuttlecock into the air and keep it aloft by using your toe, heel, and sides of your foot. Keep score by counting how many successful kicks you can do. Two or more players may also play with the shuttlecock.

Shuttlecock—China, Japan, Korea *(cont.)*

After one player tosses the shuttlecock into the air, it is kicked between the players until a player misses his or her kick. If a player lets the shuttlecock fall to the ground, then he or she is eliminated. The game continues until only one player remains.

A variation of this game is called Battledore. It is similar to Shuttlecock except the players use Ping-Pong paddles to keep the shuttlecock airborne. All of the above rules remain the same.

How to Make a Shuttlecock

Follow these instructions to make your own shuttlecock.

1. Paint a two- to three-inch (5–7.6 cm) cork ball with wood primer. Allow it to dry.

2. Sand the ball lightly and apply a colorful coat of paint. Allow it to dry.

3. Use an awl to poke 8–12 holes into the ball.

4. Collect or purchase long chicken feathers. Fill each hole with an all-purpose glue and insert the feathers, one at a time, into the holes. A few downy feathers added to the long feathers creates a nice finishing touch.

Schmerltz —United States

Equipment:

a schmerltz ball (see below)

Where to Play:

indoors or outdoors

Number of Players:

any number

Directions:

The roots of this activity are hard to trace, but many children growing up in urban America have played a variant of this game. To create a schmerltz ball, fill an old sock with sand or a tennis ball. Knot the open end of the sock or tie it with twine just above the contents. After constructing a schmerltz ball, one can invent a variety of activities to go along with it. The following is just a partial list:

- Toss the schmerltz into boxes. Use boxes of various sizes placed at different distances, and assign points according to the difficulty of the tosses.

- Compete with other players for distance or height tossing records.

- Use old tires standing on end, lying down, or rolling as targets.

- Play catch with a schmerltz.

© Teacher Created Materials, Inc.

Achi—Ghana

Equipment:
- a game board
- eight game pieces (coins, pebbles, beans, etc.)

Where to Play:

indoors

Number of Players:

two

Directions:

Before the game can begin, the players need to draw a game board using the diagram below. Each player begins with four game pieces. The players take turns placing one piece at a time onto an empty point anywhere on the game board. When all eight game pieces are on the board, the players will take turns moving one piece at a time along a line to an empty point. The object is to get three pieces in a row. The first player to do so is the winner.

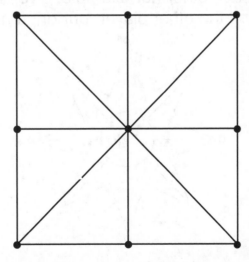

Mu-Torere—New Zealand

Equipment:

- a game board

- eight game pieces of two different colors or shapes (coins, pebbles, beans, etc.)

Where to Play:

indoors

Number of Players:

two

Directions:

This game is from New Zealand and is of Maori origin. Before beginning the game, the players need to draw their own game board by replicating the diagram below. The points of the star are called *kewai,* and the circle is called the *putahi.* Give each player four playing pieces. Make sure that the two sets of game pieces can be distinguished from each other (for example, give one player four dried pinto beans and the other player four dried navy beans).

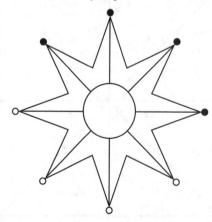

Mu-Torere—New Zealand *(cont.)*

One player starts with four pieces placed on the black *kewai,* and the other player places his or her pieces on the white *kewai.* The player on the black kewai moves first, and the players move alternately.

There are three types of moves:

1. A player may move a piece from any of the *kewai* to the next.

2. A player may move a piece from one of the *kewai* to the *putahi,* as long as the opponent has one (or both) of his or her pieces on either side of the player's piece.

3. A player may move a piece from the center to any of the *kewai.*

A game piece can only be moved if it is moving to an unoccupied point. There may not be two game pieces on the same point. The goal of the game is to block one's opponent so that he or she cannot move at all. The first player to do so is the winner.

Le Vieux Garçon—France

Equipment:
- a deck of cards

Where to Play:

indoors

Number of Players:

three or more

Directions:

In this game there are no winners—only a loser. The object of the game is to get rid of all of one's cards by laying them down as matched pairs (for example, two aces or two threes). A normal pack of 52 cards is used, but three cards are removed, the jack of hearts, jack of clubs, and jack of diamonds. The entire deck of cards is dealt out facedown, one card at a time. Some players may end up with one more card than the others, but this is not important. Each player picks up and looks at his or her cards without letting the others see them. He or she gets rid of all pairs of cards with the same value by placing them face down on the table. If he or she has three cards of the same value, only two may be discarded, and the third one must be held in his or her hand. If the player has four of the same value, then they may all be discarded as two pairs. When this is done, the player to the left of the dealer fans out his or her own cards facedown and offers them to the player on his or her left. This player on the left then takes one of the offered cards. If the taken card forms a pair with any of the cards in his or her hand, then those two cards may be discarded. This continues around the circle until all of the players have managed to pair and discard all of their cards. However, one player will be left holding the jack of spades. This person is called "le vieux garçon" or "old boy (the loser)."

 © Teacher Created Materials, Inc.

Tac Tix—Denmark

Equipment:

- 16 toothpicks (Matches are traditionally used to play Tac Tix, however, for safety purposes, toothpicks are substituted in this game.)

Where to Play:

indoors

Number of Players:

two

Directions:

Tac Tix is a Danish game invented by Piet Hein, a mathematician, inventor, and poet. He also invented the board game of Hex. To begin the game, 16 toothpicks need to be arranged in a square formation (four four columns).

The players alternate taking turns. The first player takes one or more toothpicks from any one row or column, but the toothpicks taken have to be adjacent, with no spaces in between. For example, suppose that the first player takes all four toothpicks from the second row. The second player may then take any number of adjacent toothpicks from one of the other rows, but he or she is now unable to take the three remaining toothpicks from any of the columns because of the gap—he or she may only take any one toothpick or the lower two. The game is won by the player who forces his or her opponent to take the last toothpick. It is pointless to play so that the winner is the player who takes the last toothpick, because then the second player can always win by playing symmetrically opposite the first player. For more advanced players the game can be played using a 5 x 5 or 6 x 6 square instead of the 4 x 4 square in this example.

Fan Tan—China

Equipment:
- a game board
- a bowl of dried beans
- a stick
- a stake for wagering (such as game markers or pebbles) for each player

Where to Play:

indoors

Number of Players:

any number

Directions:

This game is popular in Chinese communities throughout the world. Before the game begins, a simple square playing board must be made. Any flat playing surface with the corners marked 1, 2, 3, and 4 can be used. Choose one player to be the banker. He or she places a handful of beans in the center of the game board. Each player places a wager on one of the corners. With a stick, the banker counts off the beans in groups of four. The number of beans in the last group (1 to 4) determines who wins and loses. For example, if a player placed his or her stake on the corner marked 3 and the last group of beans adds up to 2, then this player loses his or her wager.

© Teacher Created Materials, Inc.

Backgammon—England

Equipment:
- a backgammon board
- 30 counters
- four dice

Where to Play:

indoors

Number of Players:

two

Directions:

Backgammon is an exciting and fast moving game. It is a racing game which uses counters (pieces) and dice. Although the moves in backgammon are dependent on the outcome of the throw of the dice, it is a game of almost pure skill. The outcome of a single game may, to some extent, be determined by luck, but over time the element of luck is negated and the most skillful player will most certainly win.

Each player is given 15 pieces and two dice. The players are traditionally called Black and White. In some modern game sets, the players may be any two contrasting colors. The board is divided into four sections known as tables. Each table contains six long, tapering points which are alternately colored red and white. The only significance of these colors is that they contrast, making it easier for the players to visualize their moves.

Backgammon—England *(cont.)*

The two inner tables are separated from the two outer tables by a strip known as the bar. The object of backgammon is to be the first player to move all of one's counters around the board into one's inner table and from there to take them off the board (this is referred to as bearing off). For clarification while learning the rules, the following diagram has the points on the board numbered, but these are not normally printed on the board.

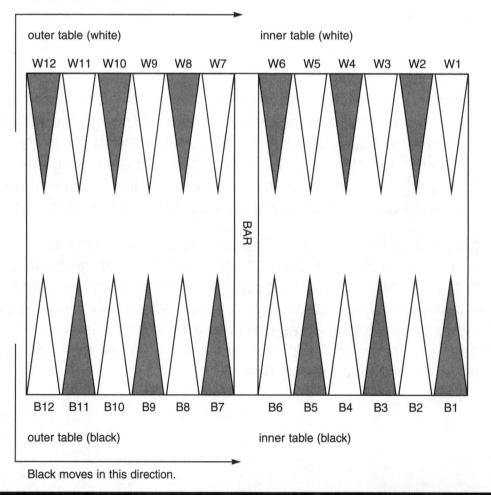

White moves in this direction.

outer table (white)   inner table (white)

W12 W11 W10 W9 W8 W7   W6 W5 W4 W3 W2 W1

BAR

B12 B11 B10 B9 B8 B7   B6 B5 B4 B3 B2 B1

outer table (black)   inner table (black)

Black moves in this direction.

Backgammon—England *(cont.)*

To begin the game and to decide who moves first, each player rolls one of his or her dice. In the case where both dice show the same number, the players should roll again until two different numbers are showing. The player with the highest number goes first and should move his or her pieces according to the numbers on the two dice just thrown. For example, if White throws a 4 and Black throws a 1, then White has the first move and his or her throw is considered to be 4-1. From then on the players take alternate turns, rolling their dice and moving their counters accordingly. After a player has thrown the dice and made a move, it is a rule of etiquette that the dice be left standing until the opponent has done the same. The basic idea of this game is for each player to race his or her opponent into his or her inner table. When a player throws the dice, the numbers shown are not added together but taken separately. For example, if a player throws a 5–2, there are three movements that can be made:

- One counter may be advanced 5 points, and another counter may be advanced 2 points.
- One counter may be advanced 5 points, and that same counter may be advanced another 2 points.
- One counter may be advanced 2 points, and that same counter may be advanced another 5 points.

If a player can use only the number shown by one of his or her dice, then the other number is disregarded. When a player can use the number shown on only one of his or her dice, this occurs because of something which is referred to as a *closed point.* If a player has two or more men on a point, that point is said to be *closed.* If a point is not occupied by either players' pieces, then it is said to be *open,* and either player may play a piece onto that point.

Backgammon—England *(cont.)*

There is no limit to how many of one's own pieces may be accumulated on a point. If a point is occupied by two or more of the opponent's counters, then it is said to be *blocked,* and the other player cannot land on it. If it is possible for a player to use one number or the other, but not both, then he or she must use the higher number. Throwing doubles is very desirable because it gives the player the opportunity to move twice the values shown. For example, a double 6 gives a player four moves of 6 points each. If a point is occupied by a single counter, that counter is known as a *blot.* If a player lands his counter onto a point occupied by the opponent's blot, the blot is then said to be *hit.* It is then removed from the point and placed on the bar. While a player has a counter on the bar, he or she is unable to move any of the other counters. To get a counter off of the bar and to enter into the opponent's inner table, a player must throw a number corresponding to an open point or a blot. If, for example, White has a counter on the bar and he or she throws 2-3 and the points B2 and B3 are occupied by Black, then White's throw is void and he or she cannot move. However, if Black has a blot on B2, White can enter on that point, hitting the Black blot and sending it to the bar. White could then use the 3 to move the same counter or another counter. Both players can have any number of counters on the bar at the same time. To be able to start bearing off pieces from the board, a player must first have all 15 pieces inside his or her own inner table. In order to bear a piece off of the board, one must throw

Backgammon—England *(cont.)*

the corresponding number on one of the dice. For example, if White throws 4-2, he or she may take off a piece from W4 and another from W2. Or, alternatively, this player can use all or part of the throw to move the counters inside his or her inner table. On a throw of 4-4, for example, White might move a counter from W6 to W2, move another from W5 to W1, and take off two counters from W4.

In order to bear a piece off of the board, it is not always necessary to throw the exact number. If a number is thrown that is higher than any point on which the player has counters left, then he or she can move the counters from the highest occupied point. For example, if Black is left with pieces only on the points B4, B2, and B1 and throws a 5-3, then he or she may move from B4 and B2. If a player's blot is hit while he or she is in the process of moving counters off of the board, that counter must be re-entered from the bar into the opponent's inner table first and then be moved around the board into his or her own inner table before the player can continue bearing off. The winner is the first player to bear off all of his or her pieces. The loser has the potential to lose not just one game but a double or triple game. This is determined by the number of counters that have been removed from the board. If the loser has removed one or more of his or her counters, he or she loses a single game. If the loser has not removed any counters, then a *gammon,* or double game, is lost. If the loser still has one or more counters left on the bar or in the winner's inner table and has not removed any counters off of the board, then a *backgammon,* or a triple game, is lost.

Wari—Africa, Middle East, Asia

Equipment:
- a game board
- 48 seeds, pebbles, shells, coins, buttons, or other counters

Where to Play:

indoors or outdoors

Number of Players:

two

Directions:

Wari is a popular game in Africa, Asia, and the Middle East. The objective is to capture more counters than your opponent. The counters, to be authentic, should be seeds or small stones, but coins, buttons, or any other small objects can be utilized. They do not have to be uniform in size or color. The game board is simply twelve round depressions. The depressions can be scooped out of sand or dirt for outdoor play, or you can use a set of cups or even an egg carton.

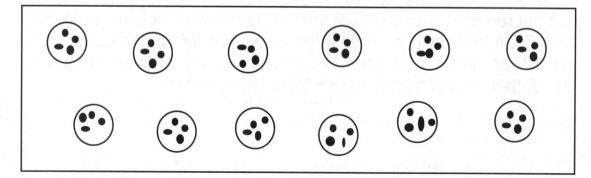

Wari—Africa, Middle East, Asia *(cont.)*

To start the game, the two opponents sit facing one another on opposite sides of the board. Each player takes one of the two rows. All 48 counters should be placed in the 12 depressions so that there are four counters in each one. Choose which player will go first, and from then on, the players will alternate turns. The player going first begins by picking up the four counters from any hole in his or her row and *sowing* them (placing them), one by one, in a counterclockwise direction in the next four holes. The other player then takes the counters from any hole in his or her row and sows them, one by one, to the right. And so the game continues.

Depending on the location of the chosen compartment, the sowing process may or may not continue into the opponent's side of the board. If there are eleven or more counters in a compartment, the player will sow all the way around the board and come back to the starting point or further, so that it is possible to sow a depression twice during the same move. The hole that was emptied, however, cannot be filled in the same turn in which it was emptied. If this happens, one must skip over it and continue to sow beyond it.

To capture all of the counters in an opponent's compartment, the last counter sown must fall into an opponent's compartment where there are two or three counters. The player who has captured these counters removes all of them and puts them into his or her reservoir (just a hole in the ground or a container next to the player, designed to hold the captured counters). A jar may be used as a reservoir.

Wari—Africa, Middle East, Asia *(cont.)*

If, after you have made a capture, there are either two or three counters in the compartment immediately preceding it on your opponent's side of the board, you are allowed to capture these as well. If you can make this move, the same rule applies to the compartment preceding that one, so long as it is on your opponent's side of the board and contains two or three counters.

The game is over when a player has no counters left in his or her row with which to make a move. However, a player is not allowed to intentionally set up this situation by capturing all of the opponent's pieces from all of his or her compartments in one turn or by making a small move between compartments on one's own side when the player could have sown one or more pieces onto his or her opponent's side. This is so the player has the honor of putting himself or herself out of the game by sowing his or her last available counter onto the opponent's side of the board.

After the game ends, the player who still has counters on the board takes them all off of the board and drops them in his or her reservoir. Then the number of counters in each player's reservoir is tallied, and the one with the most counters is the winner.

© *Teacher Created Materials, Inc.*

Pepito—Cuba

Equipment:
- none

Where to Play:

indoors or outdoors

Number of Players:

any number

Directions:

Choose two players to form a bridge by joining hands and raising them over their heads. The other players line up and pass underneath the human bridge while singing the following song.

Mama, Papa,	Mama, Papa,
Pepito se quiere casar	Peter wants to marry
Con una viudita	With a little widow
De la capital.	From the capital.
Uri, uri, ura,	Uri, uri, ura,
Pepito se casara.	Peter wants to marry.

When the song is over, the bridge is lowered and one player is caught. This player becomes Pepito. Pepito steps aside and is out of the game. The game continues until every player has had a chance to be caught and be Pepito.

The Chicken Dance—Yucatan (Baile De Los Pollos)

Equipment:
- dance music

Where to Play:

indoors or outdoors

Number of Players:

eight or more

Directions:

This dance is from Yucatan where chickens form an important part of religious dance dramas. Choose four or five players to be the jury. Divide the rest of the players into two teams. The two teams are the rhythm dancers, and they each take turns at improvising a chicken dance. While the dancers are moving, the music plays and the participants chant *"Todos somos pollos."* (We are all chickens.) The movements can be imitations of hens scratching for corn, cackling, laying eggs, or drinking water. Other imitations could be of roosters crowing, fighting, or strutting proudly. The jury expresses approval with applause. The team that receives the loudest and most enthusiastic applause wins.

 © Teacher Created Materials, Inc.

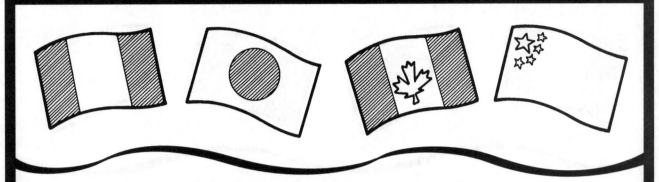

The Beggar—Cuba
(El Mendigo)

Equipment:
- chairs numbering one less than the total number of players

Where to Play:

indoors

Number of Players:

any number

Directions:

Choose one player to be *el mendigo*, the beggar. Place the chairs in a circle, facing in towards the center. Every player should have a chair except for the beggar. The beggar stands in the middle of the circle. He or she starts the game by walking over to any player and saying "*Dame pan y queso.*" (Give me bread and cheese.) The player answers "*Alla es mas tieso.*" (Over there it is harder.) As the beggar goes to another player, all of the players switch seats. The beggar tries to get one of the chairs as the switching takes place. If he or she does not manage to get a chair on the first try, then he or she must go to another seated player and repeat the whole process. If after several tries, the beggar still does not have a chair, he or she may run to the center of the circle and call *"Todos cambian."* (All change.) Again, all of the players change chairs. The beggar tries to gain a chair, and this time since he or she is not standing in front of or speaking to one particular child, the beggar has a better chance.

Bokwele—Zaire

Equipment:
  • small objects, such as stones, marbles, or buttons

Where to Play:

outdoors

Number of Players:

six or more

Directions:

This game is pronounced "bok-Wee-lee." It is a team game that comes from the central African country of Zaire. This game is played on a large playing field that has been divided into two equal halves. To begin, divide the players into two teams and assign a side of the field to each team. Each team marks a circle on the ground about 6 feet (1.8 m) wide on its side of the field. Give each team a different set of small objects. For example, one team may be given a set of marbles and the other team, a set of buttons. It does not matter how many objects are in the sets as long as they are equal in size. The teams place their objects in their circles. The object of the game is to steal all of the items from the other team's circle and carry them back to your side of the field without getting tagged. If a player is tagged on the enemy's side of the field, he or she must return the stolen items to the other team's circle. The players are not allowed to stand guard over their circles. One team wins when it has stolen all of the opponent's objects, or the game may be played for a predetermined amount of time, in which case the team with the most objects would win.

300

© Teacher Created Materials, Inc.

Wee-ichida—Native American

Equipment:
- a small rubber ball for each player

Where to Play:

outdoors

Number of Players:

any even number

Directions:

This activity is meant to be a skill builder, not a competition. It is a Native-American ball race that provides great practice activity for soccer players. The players travel either in a straight sprint or around a circular track. As they move, they "carry" the ball with their feet by making short kicks. Kicking the ball far ahead is not allowed. The object is to move as fast as possible while keeping the ball as close as possible. Try this game with different types of balls, such as soccer balls, tennis balls, and kickballs. The players may wish to race in teams, passing the ball back and forth.

Bibliography

Anderson, Karen C. *Kid's Big Book of Games.* Workman Publishing Company, 1990.

Armstrong, Cheri. *Did You Really Fall Into a Vat of Anchovies?* Cottonwood Press, 1996.

Arnold, Peter. *The Book of Games.* Exeter Books, 1985.

The Big Book of Things to Make and Play With. Boyds Mill Press, 1995.

Charner, Kathy. *The Giant Encyclopedia of Theme Activities for Children.* Gryphon House, 1993.

The Complete Book of Children's Parties. Kingfisher Books, 1994.

Harris, Frank W. *Great Games to Play With Groups.* Fearon Teacher Aids, 1990.

Miesel, Paul. *Games and Giggles.* Pleasant Company, 1995.

Schneck, Susan and Mary Strohl. *Native Americans: Cooperative Learning Activities.* Scholastic, 1991.

Shalant, Phyllis. *Mexico.* Library of Congress, 1992.

Wallace, Mary. *I Can Make Games.* Owl Books, 1995.

Warner, Penny. *Kid's Party Games and Activities.* Meadowbrook Press, 1993.

Index

Index (cont.)